The Action Man's
NO NONSENSE

Guide to Practical Fatherhood

Dr James F Slater

AuthorHouse™ UK Ltd.
500 Avebury Boulevard
Central Milton Keynes, MK9 2BE
www.authorhouse.co.uk
Phone: 08001974150

© 2010 Dr James F Slater. All rights reserved.

No part of this book may be reproduced, stored in a retrieval system, or transmitted by any means without the written permission of the author.

First published by AuthorHouse 3/1/2010

ISBN: 978-1-4490-8402-8 (sc)

This book is printed on acid-free paper.

About the Author

James Slater was born in 1959 in Fintry near Dundee, Scotland. His father was often overseas on 'business' leaving his mother, a slaughterhouse worker, to bring up the family of 3 children. He attended medical school in Edinburgh, more as a guest than an enrolled student.

He is building a reputation in the field of the psychology of fatherhood as well as breeding whippets. This book compliments a number of his other publications including 'House training children and dogs – lessons from the laundry', 'OI YOU, SIT' and 'Whoa boy!'.

Dr Slater has a number of children of his own and in his spare time enjoys deep sea fishing and photography. Moving forward as technology allows, he has developed an interactive website for children with behavioural difficulties called **www.dothatagainandseewhathappens.com** and he is currently working on a parental internet support facility which will soon be available at

www.ivetoldyouonceiwonttellyouagain.com.

In the spirit of reflective practice Dr Slater would be quite interested to receive your feedback which you can email to him at the address given at the end of the book.

Contents

CHAPTER ONE
Preparing for Pregnancy 1

CHAPTER TWO
Coping with pregnancy 13

CHAPTER THREE
The Birth 24

CHAPTER FOUR
The First Few Weeks 39

CHAPTER FIVE
Years One to Eighteen.. 52

CHAPTER SIX
Educating Your Child 64

CHAPTER SEVEN
Helping Your Child Leave Home 69

CHAPTER EIGHT
Rehabilitation For Parents 74

CHAPTER NINE
Some Other Difficult Things 86

CHAPTER TEN
Case Studies... 94

CHAPTER ELEVEN
Glossary 102

CHAPTER TWELVE
The Practical Parenting Test 107

DEDICATION

To Pedigree Chum
'Top Breeders Recommend It'

Practical Fatherhood

What the Kids say

'Buy food. And presents, job done.' Barbara age 13

'Give us the money' Dan age 15

'I've got diarrhoea again dad, I did it in your bed' Lou age 5

'He's not here, try his allotment' Ollie age 9

'The dad pays' Katie-Skye age 16

'I wish he didn't smell of fish so much' Bobby age 11

'Is this your child Sir' PC 1458 Collins AJ age 46

INTRODUCTION

Are you looking forward to being a father then? No? Neither do many men but if no one had children then eventually the bins wouldn't get emptied, there wouldn't be any people to brew beer and make television programmes and apes and Alsatians would roam the streets. The whole of civilisation would just fall in a heap. A bit like some parts of Scunthorpe really.

Eventually most men succumb to the bio magnetic draw of the procreative process and become involved in hitherto uncharted and unfamiliar emotions which are a result of impending fatherhood. These emotions could be anything from a mixture of rage and incredulity at finding the missus in bed with the milkman, to confusion and amusement at trying to figure out why your girlfriend has put on 3 stone in weight over three months and pukes when you mention 'fish supper'. It could also be bewilderment on finding out that she has spent the entire income support for January on Cadburys Cream Eggs and piccalilli.

It might even be the confusion you feel when you receive this book as a present.

In any case being faced with the prospect of having a baby, infant, or juvenile delinquent in your life is a serious business. You have two options. The first is to retreat into the swamp of pre and post fatherhood misery, lurching from one slime filled pit of parenting hopelessness to the next, floundering through a miserable and lonely existence bounded by sleepless nights and days filled with child-upbringing terror. The second is to READ THIS BOOK and make your resolve to survive as a man, a father, intact and proud.

You should notice already that this book is different to the myriad run of the mill publications on the art and craft of fatherhood. That is because this is a MANual, i.e. a book about the role of fatherhood for MEN written by a MAN. Herein are contained the distillations of many years research and observation into the whole business of procreation, women, babies and children.

From the start let it be said that there will be no deep, meaningful theorising about alcohol intake and sperm count, phases of Saturn and fertility, vitamin supplements and intelligence, breast or bottle. Nowhere will you find information on 'hair care for the expectant mum', 'mantras for pain relief' or 'how to look your best in stirrups'.

Men need good solid advice on much more important issues such as what sexual position to use to ensure your new baby will be male, David Beckham's protégé and, importantly, yours. More information is provided on mood swings, nausea, the hormonal effects of pregnancy on libido and problems associated with weight gain. As well as this there is some information on how these issues might affect your pregnant partner, wife or girlfriend.

If you are the sort of man who 'forgets' to come home on Saturday night, who doesn't notice your wife shaving her head and sharing your studio flat with four Hare Krishna devotees because you are only there in the hours of darkness then this book is for you. Even if you aren't an average bloke this book will help guide you through some of the roughest, murkiest water a man may ever have to navigate.

You can check your new found prowess by completing the self assessment test at the end of the book.

Read on, and good luck.

CHAPTER ONE

Preparing for Pregnancy

Preparing for pregnancy for a bloke starts with trying to understand the female reproductive paradigm. What this means is that women need men in order to get pregnant, at least for a couple of minutes anyway. Until women are ready to get pregnant, men as far as women are concerned, have virtually no utility at all- unless their toilet is blocked or they drive their car into a wall and need it fixing.

During this pre-pregnancy stage women regard men as shallow, gastrointestinal embarrassments, interested in 'only one thing' (cars, football, computer games, breasts, legs, beer and so on) and women will take every opportunity to make their feelings on this very plain indeed to men they have the misfortune to interact with. They largely shun the company of men and adopt a haughtiness when approached by a curious male which might remind one of a King Cobra about to strike at a Labrador puppy that just wants to play.

For that reason young men learn quickly that although women are 'quite interesting' (in a 'why have women's jumpers got lumps on the front'? sort of way) they might as well expend all their pent up energies playing sport, drinking beer and watching a bit of telly with their mates. They quickly learn that women don't understand how turbochargers and machine guns work, they reel from incredulity when they realise that women are useless at putting worms onto fishing hooks. Indeed apart from 'One Thing' women appear pretty useless at almost everything that matters to men.

During this pre-pregnancy contemplation stage women congregate in terrifying hordes, chattering about stuff men don't understand or care about (emotions and feelings, waxing, shoes, handbags, eyeliner, etc, etc). From a blokes perspective what they do and get up to in their little groups is not capable of being understood and pointless. Why, for example, do women pluck their eyelids, go to the toilet in pairs and stay in to wash their hair? These are just three examples of a whole cosmos-worth of 'woman stuff' that men will never understand, even if they could be bothered to try.

This mutual expression of 'other sex indifference' is a stable system which works very well UNTIL a woman decides she needs to get pregnant. At that point her life perspective alters course (with respect to men) by 180 degrees. As stated above, to get pregnant she needs to attract a man. To do this she uses a number of genetically pre-planned types of behaviour and some pretty complex techniques and equipment. Some of these behaviour patterns are instantly recognisable to men as 'the green light of acceptability', others are much more subtle.

Here are the things to look out for if your female acquaintance wants you to procreate with her.

- Pretending to be interested in football or motor sport.
- Not complaining when you go to the pub.
- Wearing lipstick, eye makeup and stockings.
- Asking you how your mate Eddie is and how he got on at the clinic the poor bloke.
- Encouraging you to you trade in your Ford Focus for a Toyusubishi Ninja Powerslide Monster Bastard Evo VIII Turbo.
- Waiting up for you until two O'clock in the morning when you have been out with the lads and asking if you had a nice time.
- Asking you how a turbocharger works.

You can guarantee that any two of the above examples of behaviour exhibited in a one week period are indicative of impending pregnancy.

Clearly some men don't get the option to decide when to become a parent. One minute you are watching the latest chick flick sharing a cheese and ham pizza and a bottle of Strongbow Cider and the next thing you are being dragged round Mother Care looking at prams. The whole process is summarised in the accompanying diagram.

How women get pregnant

Where there is a mutual decision to have a baby there are a number of different approaches that couples use to get the woman pregnant. The most common ones

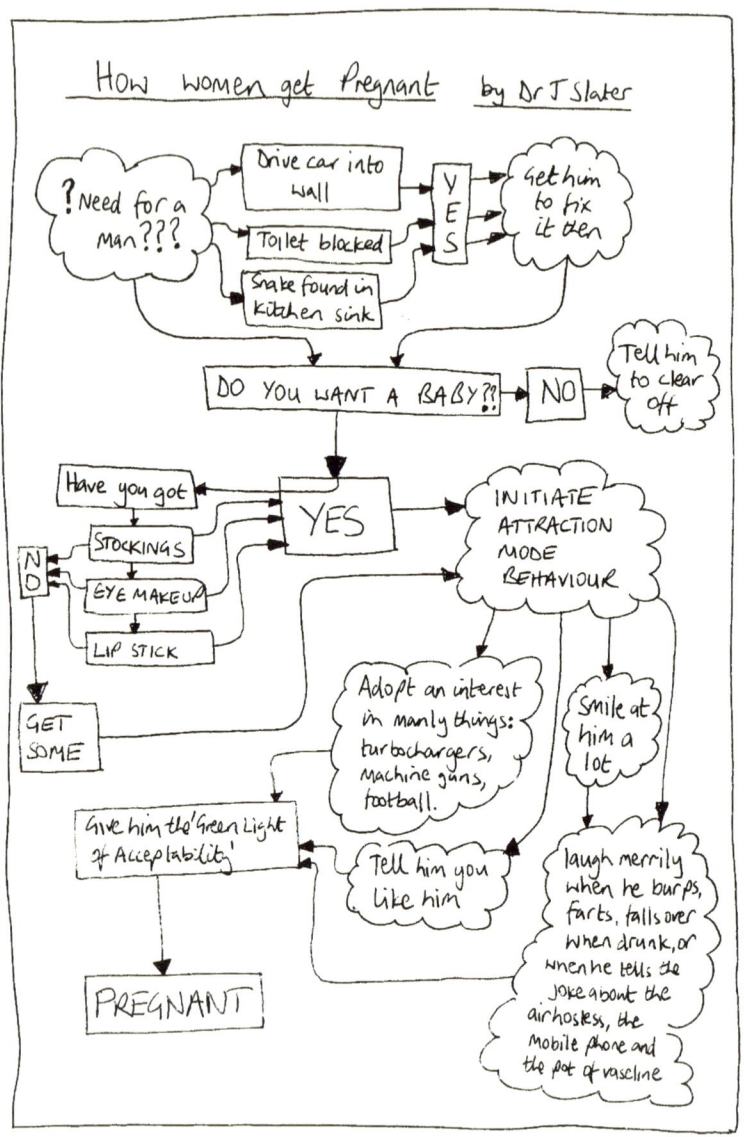

are 'The Baywatch', 'The Ford Focus' and the 'Milton Keynes' methods. They are described below. Each technique has its own merits, the Baywatch method is time consuming and expensive but makes more of a lifestyle statement to friends and acquaintances who can be involved in the full, frank and detailed discussion of the most intimate of practices.

The Ford Focus method is cheap and cheerful (in an alcohol and drug fuelled way) and avoids the tiresome deep and meaningful relationship stuff. It can be messy though but then again there are cleaning products for virtually every bodily secretion known to man, available at ASDA.

The Milton Keynes method suits those whose zest for excitement and the champagne lifestyle extends only to the boundaries of shopping in family groups for safety, wearing slip on shoes, elasticated waist trousers, driving a beige car and of course living in Milton Keynes. Sad really.

Apart from planning your conception strategy it may seem that there is little else to do to prepare for your wife or girlfriend or both getting pregnant. Research shows that this is wrong and that there are a number of additional factors which need to be considered. These include

- Diet
- When to quit work
- Preparing the nursery
- Timing the pregnancy
- Paternity issues

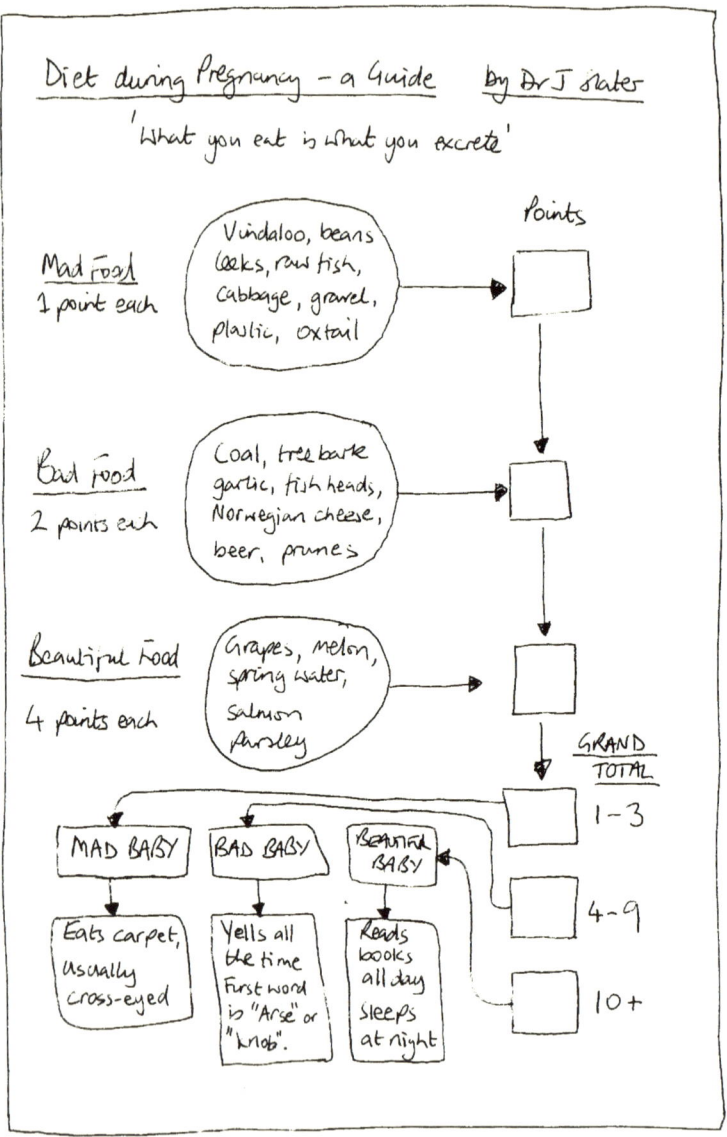

Diet.

Stavros Donner, the Greek philosopher and inventor of the kebab famously said 'you are what you eat' and it doesn't take the brains of a modern day genius to figure out just how right he was. His simple theory easily accounts for the fact that Italians have the reputation of being a bit greasy on account of the amount of olive oil they eat, the French are a bit harsh on the nose (garlic and onion based diet) Germans eat a lot of pork (enough said) the Irish eat wood and turf and the Japanese are very fond of eggs and lemon. It shouldn't come as a surprise then that diet in pregnancy is of paramount importance.

Conception Methods

The Baywatch Method

MEN

Prepare by going to the gym every day for a year
Eat beef, muesli and ginseng
Get a Brazilian, a suntan and a Maserati
Go Commando
Have sex 4 times a day....every day,
even with yourself if necessary
Ensure your partner has at least 21 multiple orgasms a
week whether she likes it or not

WOMEN

Prepare by buying Dolce and Gabbano bra and knickers
Eat Thai prawn salad and mineral water
Get a genital piercing a suntan and a cat
Have sex 4 times a day... either in person or on the mobile
After your multiple orgasm stand on your hands and get
your partner to sprinkle your parts with lavender water

The Ford Focus Method

Drink six pints of Stella, meet a pissed girl you don't know, get her into the back of the Ford Focus have a mutual grope and snog, remaining almost completely clothed get 'interested' long enough to give her the time of her life lasting 60 seconds before she pukes over you and you pass out in the heat of the moment.

The Milton Keynes Method

Have sex once or twice a month.
If you remember.

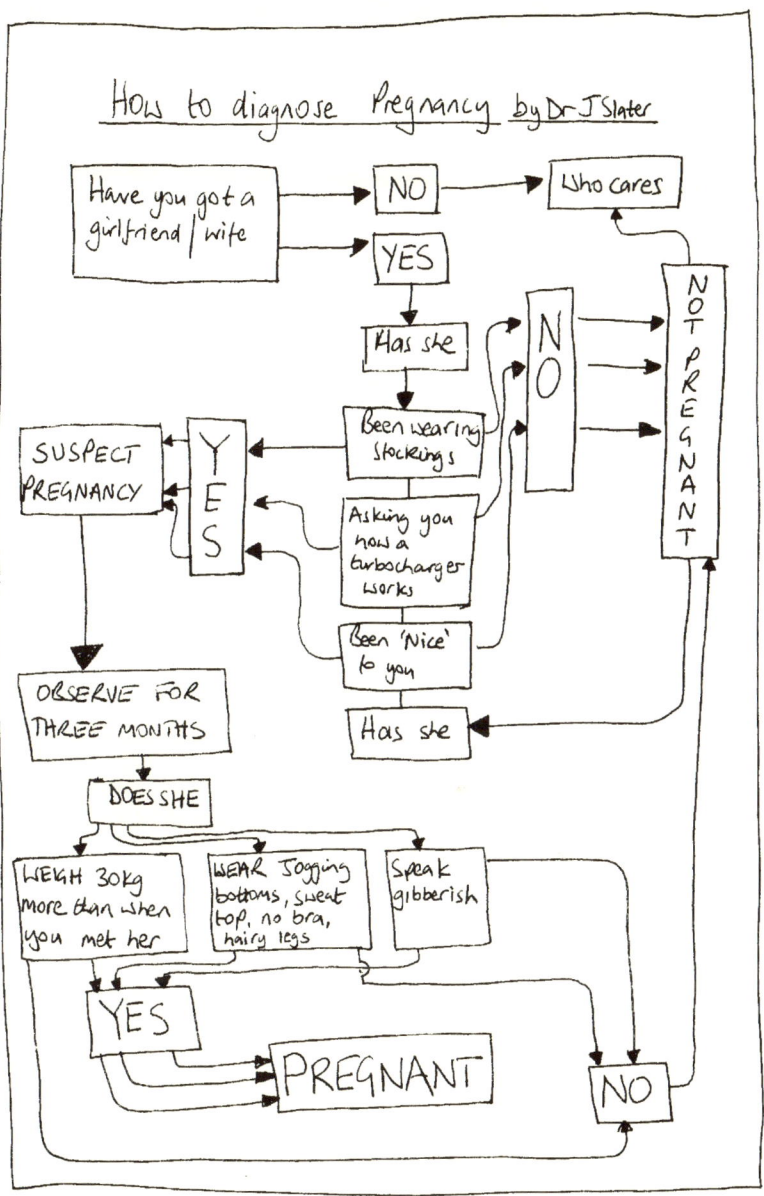

Preparing the Nursery.

Preparing the nursery is a topic second only to choosing the baby's name guaranteed to cause a maximum amount of tension between prospective parents and anyone else who believes they have a right to a say in bringing up the fruit of your loins. In general it's up to the prospective dad to get on with it though so you can take a bit more control.

If space is at a premium in your house then a number of options present themselves for the accommodation

With regard to colour schemes in general try your best to avoid colours that clash too much. A good starting point would be your football team colours, however, there are potential problems. Hugh Hind from Newcastle splashed so much black and white paint around his son's nursery that the wee bloke ended up cross-eyed. Had Hugh been a Berwick Rangers or a Wolverhampton Wanderers fan then he could have been left with permanent damage. Choose a type of paint that is washable and preferably with a pebble dash finish. The Dulux 'British Rail Intercity Unisex Toilet' range has a lot to recommend it as it has a tough durable finish combining a certain 'elegance' and 'man about train station with diarrhoea' style.

Carpet is a hazard as it readily soaks up bodily secretions and the contents of the infant digestive tract and so a thick canvas tarpaulin should be substituted.

A mobile is a nice touch but care does have to be taken. Ally Taggart from Arbroath bought a wooden aeroplane mobile for his son Jamie. Not satisfied with the static nature of the decoration he connected it up to an 11.5 horsepower motor out of an industrial stone crusher he won at a works raffle. Unfortunately the first time he switched on the planes generated a bit too much lift and he was left with a skylight he didn't want.

Timing the Pregnancy.

You are unlikely to get a choice in this matter because the procreative process is largely controlled by the female partner. However this is relatively easy. If you *are* offered an opinion try and avoid the baby arriving at Christmas, New Year, the football season, your holiday fortnight, the start of the rugby season, Halloween, Jewish, Hindu, Buddhist festival times. That leaves June 24th and October 3rd. Women know how to sort that kind of thing out. Leave it to them.

Surprise Pregnancy.

If there is absolutely no way that you could have been involved, even by email, in the insemination of your 'significant other' then you must suspect everyone. In particular it is important to examine the household accounts to try and identify if the time of conception coincided with a cheap load of coal, a missed milk bill, the time the vacuum cleaner or washing machine was fixed or the like. Be particularly suspicious of those smarmy sort of lads who appear to be taking an unusual interest in your affairs. There are some tell tale phrases to look out for which might help identify the guilty swine. Consider the following:

'Your Annie's put on a lot of weight recently, eh!'

'I see Mother Care has got a new range of nursing bras in stock'

'So…how many bedrooms does your house have?'

'Everything OK at home mate?????'

Retributant physical action should only be instigated against a suspect once it is clear that a financial gain is possible. It is remarkable how keen some people are to make a contribution to little Johnnies upbringing after a week of having dog turds shoved through their letter box.

Let's assume that you have taken the first step in spreading your genes. The news is official and all your friends have congratulated you. You now have to get on with the job of being a pregnant husband/partner and cope with the many rigors of pregnancy.

Take a good deep breath and read on.

CHAPTER TWO

Coping with pregnancy

As a man you should be glad that you don't have to suffer the physical and mental difficulties of pregnancy that your partner has to. No cheap booze, no fags, no curries, no crispy pancakes. Clothes don't fit you properly and are uncomfortable, you feel ungainly and awkward, you want to be sick all the time and you can't walk more than 50 metres without wanting to go for a pee. Its rather like coming out of the local social club at half past two in the morning to find that the whole town has shut up for the night. In fact pregnancy is almost worse as it lasts for a full nine months.

During pregnancy a woman's body changes in many different ways. The most obvious way, certainly towards the end, is in size. It is, however, a brave man, possibly a madman or an imbecile, who will enquire earnestly of a thirteen stone woman with tattoos and a moustache when she expects to give birth. The most important lesson to the uninitiated man is that fat women aren't always pregnant.

It is truly amazing that an egg and a sperm which measures less than the full stop at the bottom of an eviction order can transform a lithe, dainty, size eight slip of a girl, in a matter of months, into an eighteen stone leviathan, the spitting image of the well known Sumo wrestler 'The Karzi', or into the double of a line backer for the Atlanta City Good Ole Boys American Football Team. The really odd thing is that when the baby is born it is likely to weigh only seven or eight pounds despite a doubling of the all up weight of the mother. Explain that one Einstein!

Jock Slater, a merchant seaman from Edinburgh returned home from a six month deep sea voyage to China to find his wife who was by then seven and a half months pregnant had left home. He was under the impression that she had rented the house to a five foot one inch tall, fifteen stone, hair enhanced Turkish kebab stall owner and gone to stay with her mother. It was only after some fast talking by the health visitor who was in the house at the time that he actually recognised his wife.

The confusion lay in the fact that his wife had grown a moustache and appeared to talk gibberish all the time as well as having taken on the body *habitus* of an elephant seal.

Women's personalities also change when they are pregnant. Some go all coy and quiet (the equivalent of three treble twenties in life's darts game) and some become noisy and boisterous barking out orders for home improvements and other tiresome and expensive domestic chores.

No matter how they change, it has been discovered

that the changes are all down to one thing. Women's hormones. As any man who knows anything about women understands, hormones are the equivalent of the barbs on Old Nick's trident that he uses to prod blokes in the knackers when they have transgressed some made up woman's rule.

But herein lies a key to successfully managing the pregnant females maelstrom of emotion which can at any moment and entirely unpredictably explode into a man's world – blame the hormones. Consider the following scenarios.

You arrive home at 3.30am having had six pints too many and a bad bag of cheese and onion crisps which has really upset your delicate stomach. In effecting entry to your ground floor flat you snap the key in the lock and have to climb in through the toilet window, breaking, in the process the toilet seat. Disorientated and emotional you mistake the illuminated fish tank for the computer screen of a karaoke machine and burst into 'The Angel Song' by Robbie Williams. Enjoying yourself to the full you urinate on the wall socket next to the fish tank causing a district wide blackout and a third degree burn to your tackle. In short order your six and a half month pregnant wife rolls out of bed and confronts you in the front room. After a ten minute verbal tirade she bursts into tears. At this point you play your joker

'Away woman, its your hormones!'.

The important aspect of this is to take time to explain that she wouldn't have got so upset when she wasn't pregnant and the reason she is upset now is because of her hormones.

Likewise when she blows a complete fuse after you scorch the kitchen wall after flicking a lit fag end into the sink and it bounces out into the rubbish bin causing a minor fire. It's her hormones!

She flashes up like a Scud missile when she finds the remains of a two day old fish supper in your pillow case after you had a heavy night in the Sewer-Workers Social Club. It's her hormones!

If you play your cards right pregnancy will be relatively plain sailing using this approach. Take the example of Ian Lorne from Lancaster who reported the following evidence.

'I had my pregnant wife Betty, so well conditioned after 4 months of relatively uncomplicated pregnancy that she was convinced that her hormones were responsible when the electricity was cut off. It actually turned out I hadn't paid the bill for over a year!'

Pregnancy can be an extremely stressful time for prospective fathers and part of the aim of this chapter is to alert prospective fathers to pre-birth activities designed to strike fear into the strongest mans heart. These are the age old tribal rituals of

The Antenatal Classes
The Midwives Visit
Making a Birth Plan
Finding your way around the Hospital.

Antenatal Classes

Antenatal classes are usually where women sit on mats on the floor in massive baggy tracksuits robbed from their husband or boyfriend or partner or butch lesbian lover, practising their delivery room panting and doing pelvic floor exercises. They are generally instructed by a midwife resembling something between Vinnie Jones and The Incredible Hulk. The men usually huddle in a corner, embarrassed, staring at their shoes not knowing the difference between a pelvic floor and a parquet floor. Very little is done in an attempt to encourage the male partners into antennal class activities and this is generally for a very good reason. Men are likely to understand as much about pregnancy and childbirth as women are likely to understand about portable welding equipment and turbochargers. At the same time, while men are always in the way in any organised pregnant woman gathering they are branded as unfeeling bastards if they don't attend every single antenatal class. It's a classic double bind- damned if you do and damned if you don't.

Inevitably you will be required to attend and participate in antenatal classes, largely for the purpose of ritual humiliation by the chief midwife. You will be required to demonstrate your proficiency at bathing a rubber dummy baby with one eye missing as well as joining in with pelvic stretching exercises without breaking wind or soiling your underwear (and failing).

Avoid flippancy at all costs. Midwives can be humourless, vicious creatures as Sam Telford from Gloucester can testify. At one of his antenatal classes he was asked by the midwife how he would know if his girlfriend was in labour. With a hint of humour in his voice he replied 'She'd probably be waving a red flag, have a t-shirt with Gordon Brown's photo on and singing 'it can only get better''. This was greeted with howls of laughter from the other men present who encouraged him with calls of 'go on yourself son' and 'howay!'. The ubermeister midwife said nothing but slowly and solemnly walked past the line of men, who were becoming rather less vocal and more nervous, to where Sam stood. Without any drama she gave him a vicious backhanded karate chop to the throat which left him mute for a fortnight.

The Home Visit

The midwives visit to your home is your partners chance to show, yet again, how bad at DIY you are. Any attempts you have made to try and improve the material state of your home will be pointed out to the midwife who will add to the blackness of the atmosphere by tutting, snorting through hairy flared nostrils and from time to time laughing hysterically before shouting 'PATHETIC!!'. Make sure that on the day of the visit the house is warm even if you have to hire an industrial garage heater to do it. As far as the midwife community (coven more like) is concerned having a cold house is second only to having an open sewer running through your kitchen. If you are branded as a 'cold abode' then you can stand by to be instructed to have every manner of loft lagging, pipe insulation, damp proofing, triple glazing etc, etc installed. It won't be the midwife who pays for it either and that stuff doesn't come cheap.

Hospital Visits

The fact that your partner has to trot in and out of antenatal clinics in the local hospital during her pregnancy is another departure from the normal day to day existence of the normal man. It can be the experience of a lifetime but it also brings its own hazards.

Alan Thomas and his brother Mungo got lost in the maternity hospital in Carlisle and after three days a search party was sent out to find them. They were eventually found working like Trojans in the laundry. It transpired that they had been mistaken for a couple of regulars who apparently had turned up late for work. They incurred the wrath of the gaffer who resembled a nineteenth century harems eunuch and were made an offer to stay and work overtime that they couldn't refuse. To their credit they set a new record for complacency in the workplace and had two disciplinary actions taken against them in as many days.

On the other hand John Souness from Barrow in Furness had the time of his life as a result of getting lost in a major London hospital where his pregnant wife was being assessed for massive weight gain. He ended up working as a vascular surgeon. He was on his way to the public telephones to put on a dead cert bet on a 33-1 chance at Chepstow when he wandered into an operating theatre staffroom by mistake. When he was asked by a theatre nurse what his specialty was he replied absolutely honestly 'plumbing'. He was soon helping out with a particularly difficult operation on a bloke who had a dodgy aorta and only got found out when he attempted to replace a 63 year old mans jugular vein with a piece of copper pipe, reasoning that its pressure profile was much better than plastic and that it was less likely to freeze up in winter.

Some people never leave hospital from the time they are born to the time they die. There is a whole underworld of maniacal lunatics who rely entirely on hospital infrastructure for their food, shelter, employment and recreation. These people are called managers and executives, but that's a whole other business.

The Birth Plan

Midwives are very concerned that every woman who is going to have a baby should write a birth plan. In the case of the woman it will detail the type of anaesthetic she wants, what music she wants playing on the iPod, what incense candle she wants burning, which of her 3 birthing partners does what, and so on. A couple of examples are shown.

Men should be encouraged to have a plan of their own but this is known as 'The Afterbirth Plan'. You should carefully consider the following points. Where do you want to have the event –at home or in a purpose built facility (local pub with a kebab shop next door), what level of unconsciousness do you want to achieve during the happy event, how long you expect the confinement to be (anything from six hours to a whole weekend) and of course who your Afterbirth Partners will be and what their roles are. All details should be written down and the new father should wear a wrist band for identification purposes. Note, however, that there is now no reason to 'shave' as this is regarded as outmoded and an imposition on human liberties.

Pregnancy is a dodgy time for prospective fathers and the name of the game is survival with as few stitches as possible. Be warned though. If you think pregnancy is tough then hold on to your hat.

Next in the Doomsday sequence is THE BIRTH.

JESSICAS BIRTHPLAN

This BIRTHPLAN is to be given to all health workers who will look after me and my baby in hospital and they are to READ it and understand that it is a UNIQUE experience and I am in control.

I want the following

NO PAINKILLERS even if I scream for it

NATURAL BIRTH ONLY

NO MEN around

TOTAL SILENCE when the baby is born

My parts are to be bathed in Lavender and Honey Water after the baby is born by my birth partner

NO DOCTORS and no one is allowed to look at my woo woo

I will leave hospital when I am ready to do so

KERRYS BIRTHPLAN

I didn't ask to get pregnant

I don't want to be pregnant

I want the baby to be out before it gets sore

I want Baccardi Breezers, Morphine, a epidural (whatever that is) as soon as my contractions start

If the pain killers don't work I want a general anaesthetic and the baby cut out

I want to rest for a week after the birth and someone else to look after the baby

The baby is not EVER to be put anywhere near my boobs

I want my boyfriend castrated
I will NOT require contraception after the baby is born

BIG DUNCANS AFTERBIRTH PLAN

I WANT A THREE HOUR DISCHARGE FROM THE HOSPITAL AFTER THE BABY IS BORN

BOB, JACKO, BOB'S MATE DAVO, WARREN, JOHNNY, COLIN AND MY MATES FROM THE FISHING CLUB TO BE PRESENT

I WANT THE FOLLOWING ANAESTHETICS

GUINNESS
GROLSCH
STELLA ARTOIS

IF I AM IN PAIN THEN I WANT MORE ANAESTHETICS

IF I NEED STITCHES CAN THE BLONDE NURSE FROM A AND E WHO DAVO KNOWS DO THEM PLEASE

I WILL NEED A HOME HELP FOR 24 HOURS TO BRING ME HEADACHE PILLS, A FRY UP, ICE PACK FOR HEADACHE.

CHAPTER THREE

The Birth

Being at the birth of a child is a deeply emotional event which tends to etch itself on the virgin brick wall of memory much as a gang of graffiti artist on LSD might deface a tiled subway wall. Many have tried to sum up the essential essence of the moment they meet their child for the first time.

For example, it has been described by Murdo Thomas from Inverness as 'somewhere between an Arnold Schwarzenegger movie and a reading of the romantic poems of Emily Sweetflower'.

Wally McIntosh, an inhabitant of central Birmingham, described the birth of his triplets as 'just like Custars' last stand- the red faces just kept coming at me and then I passed out'.

For every man, the moment he sees his son or daughter for the first time will probably remain with him for the rest of his life. Take John Franks, a master eel fisherman from Nottingham for example. When asked what feelings he recalled around about the time of the birth of his son 'Wee John', a tear came to his eye, a lump to his throat and he said 'It was the best moment of my life, my mates were overjoyed for me and I almost passed out. Who would have thought it would have happened this way -a 33 to 1 outsider and the accumulator at Lingfield both came up just as Wee John's head came out. My wife was overjoyed as well and after we had gone up the Infirmary to see the new bairn me and the boys had the best night of our lives and pissed the whole winnings up the wall. Magic! ,

There are two basic types of birth, the type which happens in hospital and the home birth. It must be said that a home confinement (as pertaining to the birth of a child and not what your wife does to you when you have been on a three day rampage) is to be avoided at all costs.

Electing for a home birth is the sure fire way to attract every kind of weirdo to your house to offer support. These range from crystal and herb club activists to members of 'friends of the placenta' and various other rabid crackpot minorities. The rub is that you can be assured that usually it won't be you they will be supporting although the experience of Henry Wallis from Carlisle contradicts this. On the news being broken that his wife Hilda was opting for a home birth, a gang of latter day hippies and 'Disciples of the Embryo' camped in his back garden. He tried to evict them by driving his Mondeo Estate over their tent but they talked him round by offering him some psychoactive tea and some mind broadening fish cakes. After a puff or two on the hookah containing cerebral colouring substances he was all for them staying as long as they wanted.

So influential were they on him that from the day they left he described the whole event as 'Particularly fine, man'. His wife subsequently gave birth to a healthy eight pound boy who they named Rantantan, the Indonesian for 'man of serenity'.

Most women have their babies in a hospital. This has a lot to recommend it as it tends to be easier on the laundry bill and you should be able to get a bit of piece and quiet when you are in the house by yourself. Hospitals can be disorientating places and you would be recommended to buy a satellite navigation system and a bloody good map if you are in any way easily disorientated.

Don't be concerned by all the people in white coats, but be aware that they are not all doctors. Some painters and decorators have got away with a damned sight more than is usually provided for on the patients charter. To make sure they are who they say they are ask them about the standard of paintwork in the toilets. If you get a five minute discourse on poor quality emulsion and lack of edging technique then you know someone is chancing their arm.

By far the best option is to have the baby born in the taxi on the way to the hospital. In this way once you have established that all is well you can be easily dropped off at your local pub, thereby getting out of everyone's way in the forth-coming couple of days whilst mother and baby get the once over in hospital.

Especially important in determining how well you will cope with the birth is how well you have prepared for it, especially if your baby is to be born in a hospital. The principal and most important way to prepare is to 'Pack the Bag' The medical profession recommend that 'The bag' be packed ten weeks before the estimated delivery date.

Be cautious in how you expedite this, however. Colin Eccles from Trent Bridge ended up in the local hospital orthopaedics ward after telephoning his mother in law to tell her in no uncertain terms to get out of his house pronto. When asked why she should, he replied that his doctor had told him to 'get the bag packed' as soon as possible. He had quite forgotten that his wife's mother had been South Midlands Power Lifting Champion in 1976.

When he arrived back at his house the basic pleasantries had hardly been exchanged before he had sustained a broken arm, a fractured pelvis and various soft tissue injuries which would ensure his inability to become a father again for some considerable time.

'The bag', in the conventional sense, should contain a number of essentials. These are

Change for the public telephone to let your mates know that you have become a father and to get the drinks in.

A list of telephone numbers including the bookies (in case the confinement extends over a weekend or some important mid week horse racing meeting) a taxi firm to get you to the pub after the baby appears on the scene and your own telephone number so that you can check if your wife has got home before you have finished celebrating.

Easily digestible snacks such as pickled onions, crisps, tins of beans (don't forget a tin opener as asking for one from the nursing staff in the labour suite is likely to get you a thick ear) boiled eggs and nuts. These are essential in helping to keep your strength up throughout the whole affair. It would not be the first time that some poor bloke was too knackered to make it to the pub for his own child's head wetting. A camera is also a good inclusion in case you spot anyone famous in the hospital.

Your home team scarf to wrap the baby in to give him the best possible start as possible is also a nice touch and a sure fire guarantee to get your photo in the supporters club magazine.

Pack liquid refreshment of your own choosing. Note, however, that ring pull cans are unwelcome in hospitals as they can interfere with the electronics of the special equipment they use. This is particularly the case if the cans have been agitated in any way prior to opening and you inadvertently spray twenty thousand pounds worth of monitoring equipment with 'Auld Tams Sea Shanty Super Lager'.

Note also, if the midwife so much as suspects that your refreshments are of the 'fortified' variety you will probably end up in a bed next to your partner, courtesy of corrective physical therapy. It stands to reason that 'the bag' should be put somewhere where it won't be forgotten. Craig Campbell from Wolverhampton hit on the perfect solution when his wife, Therese, was pregnant with their second set of twins. He managed to persuade his wife to wear a rucksack with all the essential gear in it thus re-establishing a certain symmetry with regard to his wife's centre of gravity. It was less successful in bed, however, as once she managed to get settled she could only get out of bed by rolling down two planks of wood, one at the head and one at the foot of the bed. This worked for a while until she finally got tired of picking splinters out of her forehead.

Remember that 'The bag' will be your best friend during the trials and tribulations of the birth so look after it and it will look after you.

As everyone knows there are three stages of the birth process or labour.

Stage one is where the woman wakens the man up usually in the middle of the night to tell him that the process of procreation is about to come to a Vesuvian conclusion. This is possibly the most traumatic part of the birth process only second to having a Policeman's torch shone in your face as you while away the wee hours in some dark alley somewhere under a copy of the Daily Star.

Some people say that having a bath before you go to hospital is good for calming the nerves but it is a brave man who calmly tries to explain to his contracting wife that he is just off for a relaxing dip while she is screaming for morphine. A much better idea is to have a nice cup of tea supplemented with a medicinal draught of 'Old Firestarter Dark Caribbean Rum'.

Stage two is where the couple get a taxi to the hospital, get admitted to the labour suite and after a lot of shouting by the midwives the baby is born. This is where 'The bag' comes into its own. Remember that the second stage of labour can go on for up to three days and you will be wholly dependant on the contents of 'The bag' for your sustenance, solid and liquid.

If you are brass necked enough you can try to avoid paying the taxi fare by promising to call your child after the driver. Make sure you impress on him the fact that it has taken six years of intensive fertility treatment and the services of some of the most brilliant medical brains to achieve your pregnant state. If you do this convincingly enough you should even get a couple of quid for a present for the little mite as well as dodging the fare.

Stage two is where the midwives come into their own. They run the labour suite in the same way that

Hitler ran the Third Reich and you will probably not be hallucinating if you glimpse a platoon of them goose stepping around the hospital grounds under the cover of darkness. Some allow men to be with their partners and some don't, but you will be left in no doubt as to the role you are expected to fulfill whether you are invited to 'Sit there, don't move, don't speak and don't cause any trouble' or alternatively 'Trot along now sonny and leave the important stuff to us'.

This stage is complete when you are presented with you new son or daughter just long enough for him or her to start to cry and the midwife to snatch them away from you again. That's all there is to it, you are now a dad, possibly not for the first time.

Stage three is the process whereby the man phones around the relatives to tell them the news whilst toasting the arrival of the fruit of his loins in the local pub with a few mates. The secret to this stage is to select telling the news to the biggest busybody in the family in the knowledge that they will tell everyone else. This way the whole family can be informed for less than the price of a bag of cheese and onion.

The traditional way of letting the world and his wife know about your happy event is to place an 'announcement' in a relevant newspaper. For some this will be the equivalent of 'The East Midshires Sewerman's Gazette' or perhaps even the 'The Times' or 'Telegraph'. There may be different perspectives on the desired outcome depending on the wording. 'Happy Letters' are a great way to announce to the world that you have entered the realm of parenthood. These range from the begging to the threatening and unintelligent pompousness to trilling excitement underscored by rabid introspection and complete lack of insight.

If you really want to exceed all bounds of taste but maximize exposure and impact then why not upload a video of the whole thing on the internet. A transcript of a typical video diary is provided for consideration.

Some examples of these communication styles are given in the next few pages.

Now its time to concentrate on wetting the babies head and this is where your afterbirth plan will come into its own. If you really need instruction on how best to do this successfully then you need therapy. At the end of the day it's what dads are for.

The Times 28th March 2009

Gemima and Lawrence Farr-Simpson are delighted to announce the birth of Toby Rankin Beowulf, a brother for Belinda. Mother and baby doing well, major anorectal surgery to follow.

The Dagenham Gazette 28th March 2009

Jezza and Chazza have had a baybee!!!!!!!
Christowiggle-Hunka-Chunka arrived by suction on Tuesday!!!!!!!!!
Party at 64 Shedlovers Close on 3rd April
Bring a barrel!!!!!!!!!!!!!!

Exeter and District Pigeon Fanciers Journal 28th March 2009

George and Jean Morris would like to announce she had a boy on 2nd Febuary. His name is Icarus Darius. He is 7.8 kg, he is brown hair, Congratulations and thank you to everyone involved.

This is a transcript of a 'U Tube' video of the birth of Barry Trews whose father (F) had just bought a new camcorder. His mother (M) consented to publishing the words only. She was attended throughout by a midwife (N).

F   OOOOOH I can see the baby's head!
M   ARRRRRRGGGGGGHHHHHHHH FFFFFFF FFFFFFF FFFFFFFF
F   Oi Doc, can you get outta the way, I've lost my focus now
M   WUUUUUUUUAAAAAAAAAHHHH
F   Great just keep it going, just coming in for a close-up, that's really good just a few more reps
M   PISS OFF YOU USELESS PRICK!!!!!!!!!!!!!!!!!
F   Great, great, getting all the emotion now, fantastic, Oi nurse move over a bit love its not your arse I want in the video
N   Are you talking to me?
M   Keep it coming, keep it coming, BLOODY HELL ITS LIKE THAT SCENE OUTTA ALIEN!!!!
N   I said are you talking to me?
F   N N N N N N N N N N N EEEEEUUUUURRRRGGGGHHHHHH!!!!!!
M   Yea whatever just shut up love this is the good bit!

Thereafter follows a short but incisive piece of physical intervention whereby the midwife (N) renders the prospective father (F) more docile (unconsciousness)

N   Well done love you've got a lovely baby boy there, what are you going to call him, breast or bottle, disposable or reusable nappies, etc etc etc aren't men total bastards etc etc etc.

145A Churchill Pl
West Freer
Hailsham   14th December

I'm so excited to tell you all our news. Summer-Jocasta decided to be born into our world (<u>HER</u> world!!!!!!!) five weeks ago. Her birth was the most magical experience made even the more so by our wonderful friends Lucien and Hazel who chanted (naked) our special mantra for over nine hours after my waters burst and just until S-J's head appeared at the entrance to the birth canal. I can still smell the exquisite mix of incense and womb fluid. Darren massaged my perineum ceaselessly with our own secret fusion of lily leaf water and ragwort honey which meant I only had a six inch tear. When she was finally free of my body we laid her on a gemstone and crystal plinth which calmed her instantly. Her placenta was wrapped in a rush mat and sent for bio toxin analysis at the Harmonic Biotoxicology Centre in Evesham (a resource we deeply trust). When we get the results we will know what to feed her on. Of course we are keeping all her bodily waste for earth wave determination and adjust the mix of essential oils in her own free space accordingly.

Already she is communicating with us. Darren has interpreted her movements and verbalisation and she has clearly expressed a concern over GM foods. The hole in the ozone layer distresses her terribly.

She is a young lady with a lot to contribute to the future of this planet and only a blind person would fail to see her exceptional qualities. (Summer-Jocasta has NOTHING against blind people).

We would love you to come and meet her as she is changing day by day and you will deeply regret missing the opportunity to appreciate such a uniquely amazing individual.

We love her and honour her ceaselessly.

Kings
London
Dec

Hi

It's December already, and I've only just submitted the abstract for the European biochemical society meeting, don't know where the time goes. This year has been brilliant. We cloned the alpha three protease gene in February which was brilliant, this meant that the Harmer theory (1996) was nonsense vindicating the work done in Boston by Klugfield but some of the electrophoresis results which I got threw a bit of a doubt on their theory that the G5 gene activator complex was immunologically similar to the C4 transcriptor! Of course no one could believe it at first but Simmonds in Aberdeen published data substantiating my results, it makes sense after all. Naturally the gene probe studies in the llama model fitted straight in and expressed protein product analysis quite unequivocally confirmed phenotypic transformation. Double reduction sequential denial analysis sorted out the detail of whether Krebs cycle down regulation introns were fully expressed or indeed not but that's for the anal retentives to sort out!

Paul Farmer from Cambridge came to visit in May and a more fertile time of my life I can't remember. The days and nights melded into one huge genefest and the list of experiments we came up with will keep us both occupied for the next four and a half years. His ideas about exon reconstitution were staggering and when I described my plan for a glucose -6-phosphatase based vernal conjugation programme using lectin linked hybrid high pressure liquid chromatography technology linked to Southern Blot analysis he almost fainted. Fantastic.

I'm booked for the Gotenburg meeting in March and I hope the Norwegians have sorted out their P2 receptor problem by then. If not then Jurgen Errikson will look a bit silly when I present the feline seminal vesical dot blot analysis data.

Amy brought a baby home in September just before the Wirral gene hookers club annual speakers night. Apparently she also had her colon cut out in July but I was in a polymerase chain reaction half day conference at Georges so I'm not quite sure.

Simon

CHAPTER FOUR

The First Few Weeks

Imagine you are very, very drunk. Imagine you go into someone else's house. Imagine you empty all their cupboards, shelves, drawers and boxes onto the floor. Imagine, now, that you are triply incontinent everywhere. This is what your house will look and smell like for the few first weeks after the birth of your child.

As well as feeling like you are living in some kind of underground captivity bunker in Beirut there are other stresses and strains to contend with. Specifically these are, choosing a name, feeding your child and changing their nappy.

Choosing a name

There is nothing more charged with emotion than choosing a name for the new baby. This can potentially cause more domestic disharmony than actually having the new baby at home and is the cause of frequent rows between parents, between parents and grandparents, parents and uncles, parents and aunts and even parents and family hangers-on.

As in all things in life the main concern is to get your own way. There can be no more pathetic a sight than a father describing how his son and heir fought off three Glasgow policemen and a police horse only to have to admit that his son is called Lucien.

Good traditional names are what is required and that goes for the girls as well. Who could take seriously an application for an assistants job in an abattoir sluice and rest room from someone called Sophie or Gwendoline?

To help you make the right decision a list of names and their meanings is given. Choose carefully, for once the minister has give junior the quick wash-and-scrunch-dry then that's your lot. You might as well try to change the scores on the vidiprinter on Saturday Sports Round Up as change a Lionel for a Bob.

Boys Names and their meanings.

Andrew	Handyman Hence 'Andy'
Philip	Provider of plenty Hence Fill her up
James	Friend to all men
Stewart	He who understands horses. Hence Stewarts enquiry.
Edward	Literary man (head + word) or man with head like a wart (head + wart)
Michael	Man of loud voice Hence microphone
Hamish	Man who likes to stay at home (hame)
Alex	Man who trips over continually (all legs)
Bill	Man with expensive tastes
Roland	Hairdresser (from the English)
Robert	Thief

Girls names and their meanings

Morag	Woman consumed with the passion and toil of housework (more + rag)
Marie	Woman desperate to get married
Anne	Woman who is difficult to satisfy ('And ?')
Lisa	Untruthful woman
Lynne	Borrower ('Lend us five quid till payday')
Helen	Woman who is difficult to live with (Hell on earth) .
Shirley	One who disbelieves (Surely not?)
Sarah	Woman who shares
Emma	Hesitant woman
Alison	Daughter of the son of Ali

You should, if at all possible, avoid Royal names, names of countries, motor cars, pop idols, film stars, politicians and exotic culinary creations. Likewise double barreled first names are for the sons and daughters of interior designers, nail and cuticle technicians and couples who share the services of the same hair art salon.

A real problem arises when a child's mother wants a name which is trendy or effeminate in the case of a male child or just plain daft. This is where you as the father must use all your guile to prevent your family name being sullied by having an Ashley or a Timothy appear on the scene.

Open, frank dismissal of the idea is likely to be counter- productive and so the following guide should be studied.

1. Agree that the name your partner has chosen is very nice indeed.

2. Consult the following name conversion table for some example equivalents

3. Explain that to be more exclusive the name your partner has chosen when translated into the Spanish, Portuguese, Old Cornish, North American Swiss (or some equally naff language) is...

If this fails you may have to bribe the vicar and the Registrar of Births, Deaths and Marriages

Andre becomes	Alec (Old English)
Barnaby	Bob (Greek Polish)
Dominic	Davo (Australian)
Julian	Jock (Royal Celtic)
Redmond	Rab (Bavarian)
Terence	Ted (Grande Iranian)
Anastasia	Aggie (Cockney Italian)
Emma	Eiffe (Bolivian)
Natasha	Nettie (Neo Tasmanian)
Sophie	Sharon (Ancient Israeli)
Ursula	Tracy (Moravian)
Xelda	Kelly (Deep Mexican)

The Dummy Problem.

Some parents get vexed about whether they should allow their child to have a dummy or not. When most grandmothers are asked this thorny question the usual reply is something like 'I think he has got a big enough dummy in his father', an unhelpful and banal attitude to the generally meritorious efforts of dads.

Clearly the decision should be left to those who know about such things. This obviously does not include fathers. The pros and cons of children having a dummy are discussed at great length and volume at any female dominated parental gathering and this has prompted the suggestion by some fathers (usually out of earshot of womenfolk) that he will consent to his child having a dummy only if his wife will use one too.

One thing is for sure and that is they are magnificent as noise suppressor devices especially if fitted with an attachment designed by Sam Barclay of Hendon. This consists of a dummy welded onto the inside of the side of a metal bucket. A snug fit is achieved by lining the bucket with newspaper and the noise abatement properties are now being studied by a leading truck manufacturer for heavy goods vehicle cab insulation.

It is not surprising that the leading baby equipment stores do not sell these as the design failed the 'Children's Freedom of Expression Design Principles'. These are rules contrived by flower power women and limp wristed pencil necks to allow children to get away with blue murder in the name of 'self-expression'.

At the end of the day if it makes your life easier then why not go for the dummy. If you are particularly fleet of tongue you might just convince your partner that the reason the dummy works is by soothing the infant psyche. Try and get her to try it behind closed doors initially and do your ears a real favour.

Feeding and Nappy changing.

One of the ways in which it has been suggested that fathers 'bond' with their newborn babies is to take a full interest in feeding and nappy changing. Quite how a man is supposed to take a full and active part in breast feeding is beyond comprehension unless he is on hormone tablets.

By contrast it takes little expertise to make up a babies bottle and provides the father with surreptitious opportunities to 'Give the wee fella a drop of what he really wants'. It is little wonder, therefore, that some babies stagger about for ages after they have learned to walk whilst they are still taking a bottle. Likewise going back in the mists of time, fathers have been perceived to be more successful at putting fractious children to bed in the evening. As children grow up, more opportunities present themselves for fathers to share the feeding experience with their children. This can take various forms, for example, lending them a couple of quid to buy a fish supper on a Friday night or going on a fishing trip in the Highlands of Scotland with the resolve to eat only what you catch or even treating them to lobster thermidor at Rich Fellows of Chelsea.

Whilst the first example is typical of most inner-city progressive man type fathers, the second more typical of the mineral water and pony tail brigade and the third an example of the archetypal filthy rich there is one universal feeding activity which sets fathers up as the head of the family, father-provider and modern time hunter-protector.

This most ancient of rituals is called 'The Barbeque'.

This is the only legitimate opportunity that a man will get to rule the roost as far as food preparation goes. The term 'food preparation' is perhaps loosely used as the essential aspect of a barbeque is to burn to a crisp anything which comes within six inches of the grill.

Whilst most men wouldn't know or care where the kitchen in their house was, when it comes to the barbeque -only men know how.

There are a few easy rules to grasp. Only allow your male offspring to get near the action, ensure your own personal safety by avoiding dehydration (the unique blend of minerals and solutes in beer makes it ideal) and puncture the lids of tinned delicacies like baked beans with a garden fork before heating.

Nappy changing is undoubtedly a necessary evil. There is only one thing worse than having to sit next to someone else's or your own offspring on the bus after they have expunged the contents of their colon into their nappy. That is expunging the contents of your own colon into your trousers and having to sit in it until you either reach your destination or get thrown off by the driver.

The infant digestive tract is simple to understand. Put disgusting yellow and brown sloppy stuff in at the top end and out it comes at the bottom end hardly changed at all. Quite the most noxious material known to mankind, it has been used in ancient times by tribesmen in the rainforests of Cambodia as a weapon against aggressors. As a result, the tribes now tend to live far apart and the last inter tribe conflict was settled round the negotiating table with a game not dissimilar to what we know as tiddlywinks.

Prior planning is the name of the game when it comes to nappy changing. You should have at hand the following items.

Two clean nappies

A stout pair of rubber gloves or gardening gloves. A butchers apron

A face mask soaked in a quality aftershave like 'Thruster', 'Psycho' or 'Taxi'

A crash helmet in case you are overcome by fumes and fall over.

Talcum powder (self raising flour is a reasonable substitute except for boys in which case just use plain flour)

A cleaning fluid. This must be mild enough so as not to irritate baby's skin but powerful enough to strip gloss paint off brickwork.

A metal bucket with two centimeters of four star petrol in it for subsequent hygienic, high temperature nappy disposal.

You must work quickly once you have started and not stop until the safety catches on the nappies have been secured. Then whilst still wearing the essential safety gear outlined above nip outside to deal with the effluent by high temperature combustion. Do not make the mistake that Sam Holden of Whitley Bay made when due to exhaustion he saved up a weeks worth of nappies before disposal by the method described above.

Unfortunately for Sam, the nappies formed a seal around the top of the metal bucket and when he threw the match into it the whole thing exploded like a biological mortar. The result was that the nappies, some on fire, ended up on the flat roof of his extension. He was detained and arrested by the local anti terrorism flying squad for constructing an unlicensed pyrotechnic and breach of the peace. On the positive side the violent, hellfire and pungent nature of the incident managed to displace a flock of some three dozen seagulls which had taken a liking to nesting in his top story alcoves and which had been keeping him and his family awake for more than three months. The ensuing inferno burnt off most of the seagull droppings and set fire to about eight birds which took off like latter day inter continental ballistic missiles only to crash to earth in flames across town.

Two birds crashed on fire in the exercise yard of the 'Knobbly Briar Retirement Home' which was enough to precipitate the demise of one ex Army resident who thought the Bosch were attacking again as well as convincing a few others of the arrival of Armageddon.

Takensensiblynappychangingcanbeaccomplished peacefully and temperately and provides no more a hazard to health than crossing a road. The M6 that is.

If you can survive the first few weeks then you only have the next sixteen years to go before your children spread their wings. Look on the positive side, nothing lasts for ever, not even infanthood.

What Babies Think

From a layman's perspective it might look like babies just lie around a lot doing nothing, occasionally making a bit of a racket before someone sticks a teat in their mouth. Not so.

Research conducted in Finland has proved that babies do a lot of thinking and Dr Oleg Pinetree from Helsinki University has developed a machine which interprets these thoughts. Unfortunately because he is Finnish no one can understand what he says so we asked Darren Patterson from Norwich and father of three what his views on the issue were.

'I've studied this for years' said Darren 'and bugger me but it's a tough one'. The results of his studies have been put in the accompanying table.

Observed Behaviour	What the baby is thinking
Lying still eyes shut no noise	Hopefully the big people will leave me alone and not insist on shoving that massive set of boobs in my face again for a while. Ill need cosmetic nose surgery if she keeps on doing that much longer
Screaming like a Banshee, thrashing around the cot	Mars Bars not milk you idiots, AW NO here it comes again the massive mammary, ARRRRGGGHHHHHHH, oh well, just go with it.
Making 'Goo goo gaa gaa' noises	This will make the old bat leave me that three bedroom cottage in the New Forest when she croaks.
Grunting, big red face	Great, she's just stuck me in the bath and changed my nappy. Time for a monster poo. The harder I make this baby lark for them the less likely they will have another one and I won't have to share my Nintendo Wii with anyone.

Baby's First Birthday

In the majority of households there is a parental imperative to celebrate little Troy or Godiva's first birthday. Its more often an opportunity for mothers to get together to have a good old whinge about how knackering having a one year old is, and how bad their birth injuries were and for dads to talk about machine guns and turbochargers. Its also combined with a limp excuse to get on the outside of the sherry bottle.

Why not have a themed party? You could pay some psychopathic skinhead 5 foot tall 16 stone lesbian in a clown costume to shriek and cavort around the ground floor of your flat waving coloured sticks about for long enough to ensure that none of the children sleep a wink for three weeks and need powerful sedatives to enable them to stop howling every time someone talks to them.

Alternatively what about 'The Animal Man' ('Animal' to his friends) who brings along his motley collection of snakes, rats, locusts and his Jack Russell called 'Naughty Boy'.

Appearing at a titled Lady's daughters party in Suffolk all was going well until someone stood on a locust, the snake sank its fangs into the rat and the Jack Russell saw them both off, disemboweling the rat on the dining room floor. And all because 'Animal' took his eye off the ball while having a nerve calming swig from his vodka bottle. That was another cast iron guaranteed way to leave the children psychologically scarred for life.

The table below lists some party options for a range of ages and their relative benefits and problems. Expect to pay up to £150 for an hours 'entertainment' and up to £2500 for repairs to your property, fines, insurance settlements and so on.

Party Name	What happens	Good for..	Not so good for..
The dangers of drink	A 63 year old ex US Marine Corps sergeant demonstrates what happens when you drink the contents of your parents booze cupboard.	14 year old boys who like to hear 'how it really was in 'Nam'.	Vomit on the carpet. Loads of it. And M16 bullet holes in the walls.
Stuff your own dead animal	Children bring a dead animal and they are shown how to stuff it and mount it on a mahogany plinth.	Disposing of dead animals	What happens when children bring in a live animal. Like next door's cat.
How to Holler Texas style	Dook and Jolene from Bromsgrove 'Keep it Country' Club 'entertain' your kids for three hours by yelling and hollering and yodeling. Like they do in Texas	Sorry, no idea on this one. It's a real popular one with the under three's though.	Ears
Paint your dad's Jaguar	Tabitha (Performing art student with attitude and ADHD) shows your kids how to convert dad's silver Jaguar into an advert for a cats refuge.	Creativity, freedom of expression, cat awareness.	Cats when dad next sees one on the road.
Build a round-about	Steve and Jim show your kids how to excavate 8 tons of soil from neighbouring gardens and dump it in the middle of the road.	Good exercise, learn about what its like as a posh kid in the construction industry.	Callouses, non 4 wheel drive cars, preventing congestion.

CHAPTER FIVE

Years One to Eighteen

After the first year, family life assumes a spectrum of activities which all have to be coped with. In many ways the main thrust is the gradual breaking of family ties and bonds which keep your children hanging around the house. Major steps include going to school for the first time, going down the pub on their own for the first time, going on holiday with their mates for the first time, getting arrested and making improper suggestions to a police horse for the first time and so on. Hopefully parenthood ends with the announcement that he or she is off to shack up with a like-minded member of the opposite sex. This may mean wedding bells or a trip to the registry office or simply throwing a few black bin bags into the back of a taxi. This chapter provides plans for surviving a number of family events and also addresses the nature of adolescent problems. First of all, however,

Family entertainment.

There are two types of family entertainment. One is 'The quiet night in' and the other is 'The day trip'. Both can be equally stressful for the beleaguered parent.

' The quiet night in', as an organised event, requires organisation on a number of levels. The TV pages of the local newspaper need to be perused to ascertain whether a video will be required. If it is then a decision needs to be taken as to which one. Will it be 'Bambi' or' 'Death Platoon III, The Return of the Pizza Makers'. Next is the matter of food. Will it be home made (by whom?) or will it be a take away. If it is to be a take away what sort -Indian and risk the Bombay trots again, Chinese and get something you didn't order or a kebab and spend the rest of the night picking someone else's finger nails out of your teeth? As a general consideration, who will pay for it all and will Granny be invited? If a family member turns up out of the blue do they get invited to stay or do they get the bums rush? If they are invited to stay do they have to pay? Another vital question is, will there be alcohol? You can be sure that if the offer is made to provide alcohol of any type then the relations will most definitely come out of the woodwork and you will find yourself catering for fifteen rather than four or five. In short, the complications involved in planning and executing a family night in make it an entirely worthless task. By far the best idea is to spread the buzz that your sister in law is having a family night in, booze supplied for all comers and then enjoy a quiet night in by yourself whilst your squad inflicts itself on her.

The family outing is the other type of family entertainment. In contrast to the quiet night in you can actually stay in charge of this activity, especially if you are the only family member who has a forged driving license and a mate who can make false number plates. Never the less stress levels can be high, especially if great aunty Ethel or in laws are invited or invite themselves. A number of venues remain popular, especially the zoo, Tesco's and the Magistrates Court. A trip to the zoo is a chance to enlighten your family to the wonderment of the animal kingdom in all its forms. You should make the most of opportunities to draw parallels between the less attractive animals and family members who you find even less appealing. Some zoos encourage you to feed the animals, especially those animals which are not fussy eaters. Do not make the mistake of Keith Donaldson from Wrexham who got carried away when he was feeding the hippopotamus at Cardiff zoo. The more he fed it the more it seemed to want and before he knew what he was doing he had fed it his picnic box, camera and football hat. He was just about to chuck his anorak into the beasts mouth when he was stopped by the keeper who clouted him around the ear with a yard brush he had just been using to clean out the elephant house. It was two days before his camera was spotted in the hippo dung and his wife got a nasty surprise when she opened the bag it was sent in from the zoo. The photographs were sent back from the film counter at Boots with an advice sticker on each of them which said 'Incorrect storage of film affects print quality, avoid contact with aquatic mammalian gastrointestinal tracts'. Tesco's is one of the most popular venues in the summer season of family outings. It is not uncommon to see families thrill to the delight of watching wee Johnny emptying a six kilo crate of mushrooms into an old age pensioner's trolley, or flooding one of the isles with olive oil and then watch the fleet of ambulances turn up at the checkouts to cart away the hapless victims with broken pelvises.

One game designed to involve all the family in the thrill of competition is to see who can eat the most food, the winner being the one who eats the greatest amount in terms of value. A time limit is set, usually thirty minutes is enough or until the umpire (store detective) is called into play. All empty food wrappers are kept and the bar codes surrendered at the checkout for the checkout staff to tally up. The losers pay the bill of course. A day out at the Magistrates Court can be marvelous fun depending on whether you are there of your own volition or not. There can be few pleasures to compare with oooing and aaahing in tune to the description of nasty deeds perpetrated on the young, old and innocent by nasty people and whooping with delight as the judge passes sentence. Further colour can be injected into the proceedings by shouting encouragement from the public gallery from time to time. Try *'Hang the Bastard'* and *'You're goin' down and you know it'* and watching the accused relatives response, taking care to avoid being thrown out for contempt. This type of day out can double not only as family entertainment but also as an educational activity, preparing your children for appearances they may have to make in the future themselves.

Parties

Children and some adults like parties for a variety of reasons. Adults like parties where they can flirt with members of the opposite sex, drink someone else's booze to excess and not mind making a mess on the floor with fag buts, beer froth and phlegm. Children and adolescents, in their innocence, like parties because they get to stay up late, wear special clothes, play games and eat party food until they are sick. The nightmare of all nightmare for parents is when your offspring confronts you with the request 'Can I have a party please?'. Inevitably the time will come when despite all attempts at dissuasion the date is set for a party.

The age of the guests determines your approach to surviving the event. Under fives need one room containing no furniture, loads of food at one end on the floor, a thick tarpaulin on the floor and a strong lock on the door. Herd all the guests into the prepared room as soon as they turn up at the door of the house and don't let them out until their parents call for them. The room can then be steam cleaned and the damage limited to the paintwork in this one room. Six year olds to fifteen year olds can be put to some use while they are in your house. A favourite game organised by far sighted fathers is the 'Fetch and Win' game. The idea is to set the assembled guests tasks such as... 'The first person to bring me a can of beer and a kebab wins the prize' or 'The first person to clean an upstairs windows wins' or 'The first person to clean a square yard of the pigeon loft wins'. The prize can be a few cans of shandy or a swig from the vodka bottle kept by your bedside for emergency medicinal purposes or perhaps something practical like the set of Nigerian spanners which you won in a raffle once and which only fit Nigerian nuts and bolts.

Neal Crompton from Solihull played this game so successfully that he had a group of his sons friends build a garage for him for the price of a few cans of Special Brew and a copy of Gray's Anatomy which he found in a skip outside the local hospital. It was only when he found that all they had done was to dismantle his next door neighbours garage and erect it on his own drive that he spotted a flaw in the plan. His next door neighbour, however, a junior civil servant with the Department of Commerce, suspected nothing and while describing the theft of the garage to the police referred them to Neal for a description of the missing item.

Parties involving young adults of sixteen and older are best avoided by parents as they are usually noisy and oppressive affairs.

It is worth while relieving some of the guests of their alcoholic offerings with the excuse of putting them in the kitchen before nipping off down to the allotment for a quiet night with a couple of mates discussing tactics for the next dogs meeting, however.

The Biology of Childhood

There are fundamental differences between boys and girls although these can be hard to spot in the first few months of life. Clothes are the obvious difference along with the fact that boys wear blue and girls wear pink.

The Differences Between Boys and Girls Aged 8 to 13

	BOYS	GIRLS
How to play	Pick something up and throw it at someone	Organise two equally talented teams so that each team gets the same number of points
What to do with a dead pet	Cut it open and see what's inside	Write poetry and a song about how they will miss that special rat grandma rescued from the outside toilet
Favourite person	The boy in year 11 who can burp for 9 seconds	Mum
Toiletry	The Martini approach, any time, any place any bush	Own toilet, own home, own terms. Actually girls don't go to the toilet
Music	Favourite song is ' Here we go, here we go, here we go'	Favourite song is "Amazing Grace'
Favourite thing	A multi combat death-ray automatic knife tool	A lovely flower

The Differences Between Boys and Girls Aged 14 to 18

	Boys	Girls
How to play	Join a club where you can get some really cool injuries and a big scar	Playing is for children, this is for real
What to do with a dead relationship	Move on, she wasn't that good anyway	Discuss, dissect, extract meaning from, make resolutions
Favourite person	The bloke in lower sixth who can fart for 9 seconds	Me, me and me
Toiletry	Make sure to show your mates	Blokes don't know how lucky they are
Music	Something, anything that makes your ears bleed	That really meaningful song that no one knows what it means
Favourite thing	Blipper, trouser truncheon, meat and two veg	Mascara and cover-up

Problems of Adolescence.

Remember that you were once a pubertally confused individual yourself. Adolescence can be a difficult time for children as they start to sprout pudenda like mushrooms appearing on a dunghill. It is the woman's job to guide her daughters through the female puberty minefield and the mans job to explain to his sons that as long as he stays well away from girls and takes up a pastime like deep sea fishing and gets his name on the council allotment waiting list then everything will be OK. Do not expect your children to take any notice of you, however, as they will reward your years of indifference with good honest contempt.

Sex Education

This is the minefield that all parents want to avoid. But it's unavoidable and the only way to deal with the whole sordid nature is to confront it head on. There is no 'one size fits all' approach to sex education and cultural and regional influences will determine the approach to take.

Here are some examples of educative styles that can be found,

The Kensington Mum and Dad get naked at the dining table and have an open and frank discussion with their children about Tantric Sex demonstrating some of the trickier moves like 'Lion eating a Humming Bird'.

The Huddersfield Mum drags her daughters into her bedroom where dad is snoring, farting and moaning away to himself after a three day 'fishing trip' points at him and yells at the top of her voice 'If you're not careful you'll end up with a waster like that by gum lass.'

The Highlander Sex education is largely based around frostbite avoidance procedures. For this reason most Highlanders don't take their vests off. Or anything else for that matter. Sex is for Southerners or when you are on holiday in the comparatively sub tropical region around Ayr.

The Somerset 'See the bull in that field etc etc, Oooooo AArrrrrrr, etc etc, never ask a female woman of the opposite sex to have a go at threshing on your combine harvester on a first date etc etc.

Sex Education - Key Points

If you do your job right then you will equip your child for a well balanced understanding of the opposite sex. This is amazing since, as discussed previously, most blokes haven't the first clue what women are all about.

Boys	Girls
If you haven't had sex with the au pair by the time you are 15 then you are GAY	Boys are only interested in 'one thing'
Girls who don't want to have sex with you are lesbians. All of them.	Boys never change their underwear
Normal girls are all gagging for it	Boys just DON'T UNDERSTAND
Beer, curry, sweat, cheese and onion are all odours that girls are attracted to	He can hold your hand -only when you let him
Women are attracted to arses, that's why they think 'mooning' is such a masculine thing to do. It's also why they want to marry Premiership League footballers.	If he doesn't notice your Wonderbra then he is gay
Her perfect present - edible body paint and a see through bra.	His perfect present - soap and a ticket outta here

Your job as a parent will usually end when your child shoots the grot or in other words, leaves home. As happy a thought this may be there is usually one supreme hurdle to overcome. This is the wedding. If you have daughters then expect to pay through the nose for a cold, bland chicken lunch with pulverised vegetables and rubber desert. Expect the groom's family to look down their noses at you and the rest of your family, even though they themselves are little more than gypsies and not one of them has the rights to an allotment. Make sure you get all these points over in your speech so that you are not bothered with irritating Sunday afternoon visits from them expecting a cup of tea and a cosy chat while all you want to do is watch the football.

Console yourself with the thought that when your son gets married what you can't drink at the wedding reception you can happily through over guests you neither know nor want to know.

CHAPTER SIX

Educating Your Child

Far from the happy go lucky approach of the parents of yesteryear, fathers are becoming more and more involved in their child's education.

The father of today is expected to be able to provide everything from a solid, competent background in a wide range of subjects (which leads many to adopt their childs exam results as a reflection of their own intellectual prowess) to a good thump round the ear to reinforce a full understanding of family and social etiquette.

The following guide will provide you, dad and intellectual head of the family, with simple but sound advice on infant and child education, ensuring that he or she will capitalize on your own intellectual wealth. And that is worth more than gold bars.

Geography

The skill of knowing where you are, where you want to be, how to get there and whether the natives are likely to be friendly. Ensure, therefore, that your child knows the locations of the following principal landmarks, how to get from one to the other in the shortest time and back to the house before he is missed by his mother.

The Chippy
The Bookies
The Police Station
The Off License
The DSS Office
The Courthouse

It is important that junior realizes that his house is the centre of the universe and that he will be required at a minutes notice and on pain of suspension of pocket money to get to the chippy, off licence then the bookies and home before the chips get cold. Likewise he should be engendered with negative vibes concerning the police station and courthouse. Take every opportunity to explain that this is where the nasty men who steal dads dole money live and where ......and in no time he will have a fully centered disposition regarding the forces of law and order.

History

Family history is far more use than national or world history with one exception. Make sure that your child can recount the victories at least at national level and certainly at European level of your own football team. The fact that sir Hubert Hubert got his ass kicked by the clan mactavish on Flodmorton moor in 1767 is of tiny significance compared to the slaughter of St Mirren by Dundee at Dens road (4-1 Brooks, Heggary, Simpson and McFee) in the Scottish Cup in 1957.

Make equally sure that he has a sound grounding in family history especially the dates and length of sentences of convictions of at the least the last two generations of your family. Remember there is no such thing as a skeleton in the cupboard but only the colourful characters of aunts, uncles, grandparents who all did time for benefit fraud.

Science

This is a very highly over-egged discipline which can be reduced to the essential elements of
    How to turn on the TV (Physics)
    How to work the DVD (Computing)
    How to open a tin of beans (domestic science)
    How to work the microwave (Electronics)
    How to spot a bad pint (Biology)

Anything more complex than this naturally requires the services of some kind of boffin, more than likely someone who has done an internet course sanctioned by the University of West Croydon. Not surprisingly most three yearolds have mastered at least 4 out of the 5 essential elements of science listed above.

Languages

In an alien environment being able to speak in languages could save your life. Consider the following scenario. Its winter, an away match at Arbroath (just inside the Arctic circle) and although you have enjoyed the sustenance of seven pints of McEwans Eighty Shilling you are fast approaching a nutritional crisis. You must eat within the next ten minutes or die. Your team has won 5-2 and the natives may not be that friendly. Your imperative is to get into the take away emporium and out again as soon as possible before you are rumbled by the locals. Ensure your progeny can deliver the following 'behind enemy lines' lines before they are eight years old.

Indian. 'Two onion bhajis a portion of chips and curry sauce expresso please Jim'

Chinese 'Two crispy pancakes, a portion of chips and some sweet and sour sauce at the rush please pal'

Turkish 'A donner kebab a portion of chips and some of that red sauce pronto please chief'

Italian 'A 12 inch spicy beef pizza, a portion of chips and some of that neopolitan sauce NOW Emelio'

If you maintain your cool, speak slowly and loudly you should have no trouble whatsoever.

One other phrase which will eventually come in useful at some stage is 'I will say nothing until I am provided with the services of the duty solicitor'.

Mathematics.

Any average 7 year old should be able to calculate the dividend on a 33-1, 100-6 and a 7-2 accumulator taking betting tax into account.

Pets

Pets are a great way to educate children. See the accompanying table for the benefits of pet ownership.

Benefits of Pet Ownership

Type of Pet	Good For	Bad For
Dog	Companionship	Eating carpets, beds, clocks, electricals
Cat	Low Maintenance	Jittery when locked in a wardrobe for a week by mistake
Rat	Tends to eat other dead pets	Scare Factor
Tape Worm	Obesity	Repeated trips to the GP
Head Lice	Keeping other children away	The pony tail argument

CHAPTER SEVEN

Helping Your Child Leave Home

There comes a moment in every fathers life when it is time to cut the deep paternal ties which bond offspring and parent, ties built up over time much like the sludge in a chip shop waste disposal unit. Sooner or later it is time to utter the metaphorical 'see you down the pub' to which the retort is usually 'not if I see you first'. Then its time to get the 'Draino' out and flush the offensive sludge out of your system.

Put another way kids usually become such a pain in the arse that either they go or you go.

By using one of the high tech solutions below helping your child to shoot the grot can be achieved fairly easily and without much fuss. For suspected hard cases you may need to use them all.

For those fathers who think they might have a problem reclaiming their child's bedroom, dumping all their gear in a skip and reclaiming it as a workshop for your fishing gear then it's important to appreciate that there are parallels in nature. Does not the majestic swan drive away his singlets to pastures afresh and does not the regal bull slug rear up against his sluglets forcing them out of the family nest to find a slime pit of their own?

Plan A 'Please don't go my life would be empty without you'

In short you must attempt to smother the existence out of your child so that in desperation he or she clear off of their own accord to get some space of their own.

1. Ask where he is going any time he ventures out of your sight especially inside the house.
2. Ask for a complete breakdown of his planned movements for the day
3. Never be slow to point out that 'there are some very dodgy people around these days'.
4. When parting company always say in the most sincere voice you can muster 'Take care now' at the same time touching their arm.
5. Continually reinforce your deep feelings for the structure of the complete family unit by saying things like 'you'll never leave home will you it wouldn't be the same without you'
6. Always make a point of sitting up at night to await their return from a night out. Get a blow by blow account of who what where when and why.
7. After they have put their light out at night poke your head in their bedroom to ask them if they are all right, after leaving leave their

door ajar.
8. Continually ask them if they are OK, especially when sitting watching TV in silence.
9. Keep telling them how tearful you felt when you took them to school for the first time.
10. Insist on a hug and a kiss from the boys as well as the girls on seeing them for the first time of the day.

If this doesn't work after a month then move on to plan B

Plan B 'You've got your whole life ahead of you I wish I was in your shoes'.

This plan is designed to reinforce any positive aspect of leaving home.
1. Regularly ask if they are looking forward to leaving home
2. Stress what a great time you had when you left home for example 'I was pissed every night of the week for the first six months after I left home'.
3. Mention that normal seventeen year olds cant wait to leave home and that only losers and deadbeats stay at home with their parents after the age of seventeen.
4. Promise to buy them a car when they go.
5. Arrange a Council Housing Officer to visit him.

Plan C The unsubtle approach

1. When entering a room where your child happens to be immediately say in a loud voice ' What the hell is that smell'. Sniff around the room eventually giving him or her a long lingering, stern look then leave.
2. Collect all their clothes together in a black bin bag and throw it in the outside toilet
3. Change all the door locks and don't give then a key
4. Always demand to watch a different channel on the TV to the one they are watching
5. Move house and don't tell them
6. Tell them they will have to share a bedroom with their brother or sister because 'the lodger arrives next week
7. Keep telling them how you hate bloody freeloaders, parasites and hangers on
8. Pretend to forget their name
9. Bang on the door and ask them what the hell they are up to when they are in the toilet
10. Always ask if they will be home for dinner again tonight
11. Tell them that your mate Eddie said that all young people get a free flat of their own if they front up to the council offices with all their belongings, then help them pack
12. Tell them to **** off

Plan D Physical Eviction

This can be done by either yourself or a friend of yours pretending to be from the bailiffs office. Explain that as they are the eldest child they have to get out first and bloody well stay out and it's a new law from Europe

Plan E Mental Illness

Feign mental illness by acting more loopy than normal. For example you could eat a sock in their presence, start singing psalms in the middle of the night, pretend to be a chicken or use a pogo stick to get around the house. Get a friend of yours to explain that you caught it from a bloke down the road and that the house is now infected and that environmental health office has ordered everyone out.

Using these basically simple strategies even the most stubborn child will eventually crack and leave home.

CHAPTER EIGHT

Rehabilitation For Parents

You did it! You have finally discharged your duties as a parent and you can settle down to a life of patient contemplation and self congratulation. Let your mind wander a bit as you pick the slugs out of the composter at the allotment and casually flick them onto the bloke next doors cabbage plants. And remember your proudest moments.

Parents Proudest Moments

Proudest moments are the diverse memories chiseled into your memory and of course parental perspectives are very different. Have a look at the following table and see if you can identify with any of the sentiments expressed. This is of course a way to relive your youth through your children and pubs countrywide are filled with proud parents who delight in describing how little Eric age six gave the Police the slip after tossing a firecracker into the local library etc etc.

Despite the pride, underwear-soiling terror and angst you have experienced as a dad it is unlikely you will ever get back to normal. As your children, particularly the girls, get older they start to assume the highly psychologically damaging nagging aspect of the psyche of their mothers. Likewise sons can develop tendencies to compete with the past achievements of their fathers and this is particularly trying when your best feat was, and still is, navigating your way home from the pub after ten pints of Tennant's Super and a kebab.

Even after your children have left home, and lets face it not all do (especially the ones no one else will have) they can still exert pressure, all the more concentrated during visits at weekends, holidays, and when they forget where their own home is.

This continual intrusion into your life after adolescence is bad news. It is the single most important reason for developing a life and interests of your own as soon as your children show the vestiges of independent thought. These interests should be developed around getting yourself out of the house as much as possible and the vehicle for this is most usefully an allotment. But there are other options as well and they are considered below.

Parents Proudest Moments

Age	Dad	Mum
0 to 1	The time he puked over your mother in law	That first smile
1 to 4	The first day he goes for a little toddle outside and doesn't stand in a dog turd	That first word 'Mamma'!
4 to 10	His first school expulsion for standing up for the concept of free speech	Her first day at school when she is chosen to be Nature Table Monitor
10 to 15	The day he blocked the toilet and you had to call out the 'Major Mud' Team from 'Snake-O-Rod' drain engineers	First time she cooks breakfast for the family
15 to 21	The night he drank six pints of lager and didn't need the toilet or a stomach pump.	When she dated a Swedish Banker whose father is single, six feet tall and offered you a shoulder rub
21 to 40	The day he gets divorced and goes to live on a yacht in the Mersey with his German Shepherd.	The day she married a millionaire businessman on death row in Nevada because she KNEW he was innocent

The Allotment

Be well assured that you need not have any interest whatever in the ancient and noble art of gardening to enjoy the thrills, spills, peace and quiet and womb like security that a man can experience in his genetic right to enjoy his allotment. You do not need to get down and dirty with horse manure, trowels and bone meal (what????) to maximize the effect of an allotment on your post parental rehabilitation.

In this way the routine of old ie maintaining a presence in your own house only in the wee hours or at a time to suit yourself can be regained. Undoubtedly you will meet other poor sods in the same situation as yourself and you can look forward to spending the rest of your life debating the pros and cons of family life. Such as it exists. Hereafter lie many opportunities for moaning and whinging and even swapping plans and ideas for the mutual enhancement of the lot of those who have graduated to fatherhood.

Considering now the specifics of the world of allottmentational practice there are a number of requirements aptly described by Bernie Cummings, an ex window cleaner and part time sewerman's assistant from Exeter 'An allotment without a shed is like a three legged greyhound, at the very least an embarrassment and at best a bloody nuisance'. There is only one feature of the allotment which of paramount importance. The perihelion of allotment constitution, structure, order, and place in the paternal universe is THE SHED. It does not matter one brass razoo whether the allotment is only one square yard bigger than the shed as long as you have a shed.

A wooden shed is best and a window is a useful accessory but by no means compulsory. The door needs a lock on the inside as well as the outside, you need to be guaranteed total seclusion when you require it.

Ensure that your shed has all the essential comforts of home with none of the detriments. A radio, kettle and approximation to a bookies shop would be ideal. On no account should you have a TV, fridge, or bed. Such accoutrements are like a three day old kebab to blue bottles as regards tramps, down and outs, ner-do wells and other undesirables who will be attracted to such available luxury.

One man, remaining anonymous due to issues of national security, refurbished his 1986 B and Q 'Old Alaskan' model shed with the winnings of a fine night at the dogs. He installed a window, chemical toilet and put down some carpet rescued from a skip out side the local health inspectors' office. In no time at all he had a family of Irish itinerants living there after he came back from his holiday on the Isle of Man. It took him three weeks to get them out, achieved only after he stuffed a wasps nest in through the window. He was left with a shed in a worse state then when he started.

On the plus side they did tarmac the entire allotment negating any further tedious and distracting plant or vegetable cultivation type activity.

How better off would he have been had he invested in Guinness or Theakston's Old Peculiar and then pissed the whole winnings up the wall with his mates in a phone box of his choice.

Make certain you choose an allotment where the ground has been poisoned to obviate the need for continual justification of the lack of stuff you grow there. You can achieve this by pouring petrol, diesel or old sump oil all over the place, best done in spring before the delicate shoots of new growth burst forth. It also stops foxes befouling your territory.

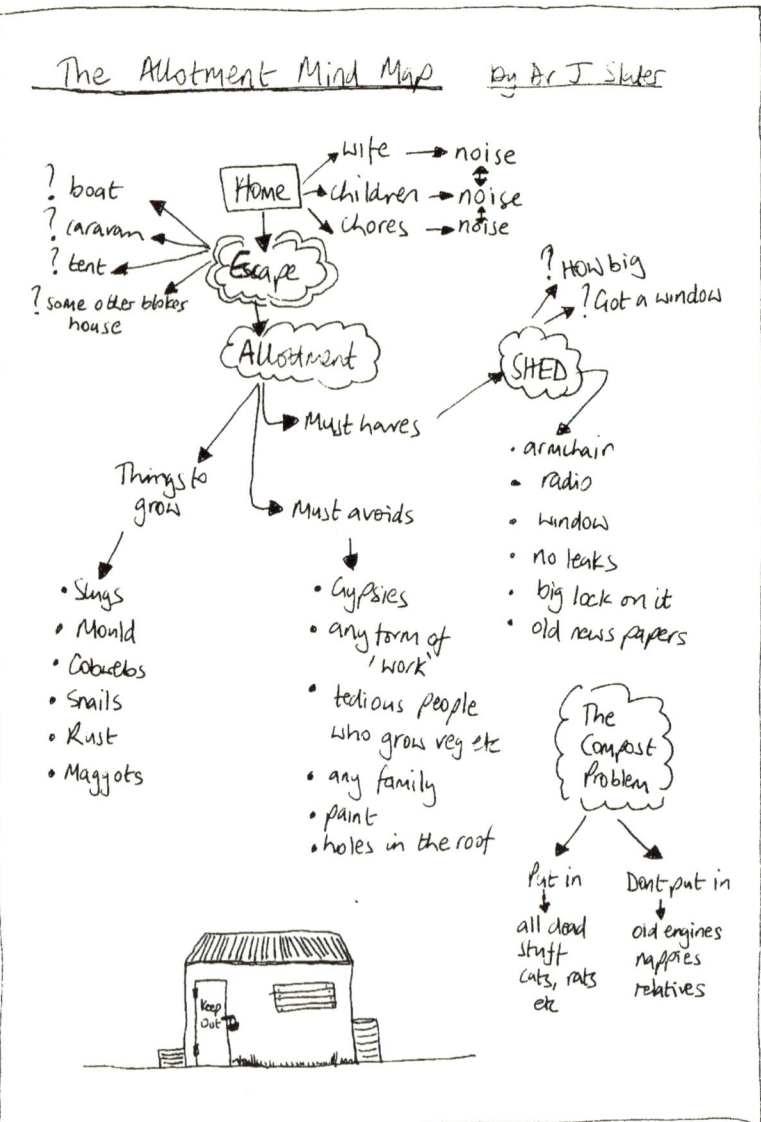

Shed Rules

Never take your boots off in another mans shed

No anal expungement in another mans shed unless the owner tears one off first

Never appear topless in another mans shed

No gobbing off, boasting or politics to be discussed

No football paraphernalia

No politicians, 'celebrities' or children under 17 allowed. Ever

Bring a bottle, or six cans, or cider, sherry. Whatever.

Fishing

Fishing is another noble pastime which you can resort to but it does have its disadvantages. Do bear in mind that all your time will be spent out of doors as a rule fishermen have a special 'odour' about them. However, as a getaway from it all activity, it has it all.

Seth McManus from Whitby used the excuse of 'high seas' to excuse his inability to maintain continence and stand up by himself on most Sunday mornings after his Saturday fishing trips for quite some years. The truth of the matter was that him and his pals used to make a bee line for 'The High Seas Cocktail Lounge and Spanner Shop' first things on Saturday mornings. The closest they ever got to catching fish was buying prawn cocktail crisps from Big Eddie the barman.

An alternative approach for the enjoyment of the pursuit of man against fish and family and at the same time getting a bit of time to himself was contrived by Norman Underwood from Prestonpans. Committed to the upkeep of his tackle and the production of high quality bait he established a workshop in the disused coal shed in his back yard. His simple strategy for keeping his family out of his space was to breed maggots. His family didn't suspect that he didn't breed maggots judging from the smell emanating from behind the door but Norman kept them guessing as to their size and ferocity. Describing them as 'like Cumberland sausages with teeth' he enjoyed solitude for years until the coal house was blown down in a winter storm.

To maintain the mystery of his hobby he went into seclusion for a week mourning the loss of his 'Queen Maggot' which he told everyone had been killed by a falling breezeblock. In fact the Queen maggot was nothing more than an old bicycle tyre inner tube which had been spotted by his four year old daughter Stacy. Being grilled by his wife he explained that by the time Stacy had spotted the corpse of his lynchpin maggot it had all but rotted away to its foul and fetid innards. He also took the opportunity to explain that he would have to travel to Huddersfield to see a specialist maggot breeder to get a replacement thereby spending a bit more time away from home on a few benders with his pals.

On his return he only had to hint at the success of his trip by exposing the tip of a moldy courgette from under his donkey jacket to ensure they would stay away from the new hatchery which he constructed by reversing an old Post Office Transit van into his yard and painting the windows black.

Photography

Photography is a pastime which can appear high tech and expensive but is another way of spending ours of solitude in a non challenging dark and warm environment. A dark room is required and this can be most easily accommodated in the attic or basement of your house. The success of the darkroom does not depend on the size of your enlarger, the light tightness of your door or the number of times a week you change your processing solutions. It simply depends on the size of the red light you have on the door to warn people to keep out.

Phelim Attwood from Derby told his family that if they entered his darkroom when the light was on that he would get a massive dose of radiation from his equipment resulting erratic behaviour and excessive hair growth. Like a werewolf. This worked brilliantly for years even though the only 'equipment' he had was an old extractor fan he used to disperse the fumes coming from his home brew set.

Far from being a sedentary pastime, photography requires the enthusiast to get out of his usual environment at regular intervals. In fact photographic assignments usually extend over a number of days and often need a mind freeing intake of beer to make a complete success of things. Here is a list of assignments and what they can usefully entail.

Photographic Assignments

Assignment	Details
Wildlife	Three day meeting at the local dog track staying in your mates camper van, eating raw chillis and jerky
Humanity	Three day assignment in the local licenced hostelries studying 'people'
Landscape	Sleeping rough in a ditch on the outskirts of town after a two day bender in the local British Rail 'Clipper Bar'
Still Life	Attendance at your local football teams 6 nil defeat by a girls team
The Human Form	A lads night out at the local topless bar
The Last Frontier	A sea fishing trip surviving on Kwells and Guinness
Drama	Attendance at the local A and E department, followed by the police station after a fracas

What should you do when challenged by the total lack of photographs to show after 'working' so hard? Simple, explain that until your portfolio nis complete you have to keep all photos under lock and key to preserve copyright. Alternatively explain with a pained look on your face that artistic talent can't be turned on and off like a tap.

Foreign Language

Most women suspect their husbands speak an unknown foreign language after a few refreshing ale based scoops. This is open to the alternative interpretation that women *listen* in a different language to men.

Remember you deserve a pastime after what you've been through as a full on action man dad.

CHAPTER NINE

Some Other Difficult Things

Fatherhood, its duties and responsibilities, is such a massive human task that even this detailed and comprehensive tome cannot hope to cover every single topic. However, there are some particularly knotty issues which can un-nerve the first time dad. Don't panic, stay calm and read on. You need to be comfortable with the following

>Childhood First Aid
>Infant Folklore
>The Problem Pages

First Aid and Childhood Illnesses

First Aid is a skill that every dad should have some knowledge of since accidents in and around the home are really common. More common than you'd expect to find on an OAP's outing to the local ice rink sponsored by Vladornoski Spine Stunner Vodka. You would be well advised to consult a more mainstream first aid manual for the detailed official way to put a plaster on a septic thumb but here are a few common problems you need to be up to speed with.

Dog Bite. You will be on a very sticky wicket indeed if your child bites another blokes dog intentionally or by accident. Clean the area thoroughly and consider taking the dog to the vet to be immunized against infant influenza, baby bubonical fever and toddler tendinolysis. Compensation may be liable to the dogs owner, consider limiting this by an immediate offer of a weekend in your shed on the allotment, with the contents of the fridge thrown in.

Car Accidents. These are commonly caused by the child's inability to reach the steering wheel while in charge of runaway cars. The bottom line is that if you do leave you child in the car while you nip into the corner shop for a pound of sausages then make sure it is properly immobilized. Try locking your child in the boot.

Infectious Diseases. Children are great breeding grounds for all sorts of diseases and are even better at spreading them around. Therefore, after someone else child has been in your house its time to break out the germ warfare kit. Bleach and whisky. Drink the whisky and throw the bleach over all surfaces. Don't get this mixed up or you will end up in A and E with the cleanest colon known to man and never being able to look at yourself in the mirror for having wasted the fathers universal cure all.

Sore Ears. Usually the result of a particularly vocal six month old being fed too many 'E' numbers. Prevention is the best policy here, wear ear defenders when you are within six feet of a baby. You can also drown out some of the more damaging high frequency noises that children emit by playing Motorhead at full volume in your maisonette. If hearing damage has taken place then you should undertake a prolonged period of recuperation down at the allotment.

Sore Throat. Usually caused by over vigorous and prolonged verbal disciplining. If you are in the habit of having to call your child to bring a copy of exchange and mart to the outside karzi after a night on the vindaloo and this extra strain hurts your voice then consider buying a megaphone.

Depression. An inevitable consequence of fatherhood. Good solid support from like minded pals down at the allotment is the way to deal with this, but some blokes never recover and end up with jobs such as bank managers and tax officials the miserable bastards.

Passive smoking. If your seven year old must smoke then try to keep them off the stronger brands like 'Moroccan Collapsers' 'Miners Windpipes' and 'Jolly Jack Tar Bronchials' Passive smoking can not only affect the health of other humans in the house but also animals as well. Father of smoking triplets Eric Maundsley from Wallsend had to have his 2 alsations on a constant oxygen supply when the triplets turned nine. Whilst the oxygen cylinders were not cheap the main expense was in the miles of gas tubing he needed when he took the dogs out for a walk. And replacing the roof on a regular basis when the oxygen periodically exploded. It took some time for him to convince the triplets not to stub their fags out on the settee.

Teething. A problem for all fathers, this troublesome issue can lead to the destruction of furniture on a grand scale. Special unpalatable paint can be bought to spray on furnishings which repels toddlers. This can be bought from most council offices and was originally developed from Ozzie Dans Dingo Spray. Its main constituent is Koala dung which can add a certain antipodean atmosphere to your home.
Much more severe precautionary measures must be taken for toddlers with a full set of teeth and particularly for those that can crawl and climb. Selwyn Evans from Prestatyn described the scene waiting for him when he left his son and daughter both under three years old alone in his flat while he nipped next door to borrow a roll of toilet paper. 'It reminded me of one of them David Attenborough films where the locusts eat all the crops in Africa. There wasn't a bit of furniture which hadn't been shredded. I had to go next door again to borrow my neighbour's mobile to phone the social services for a crisis loan to buy new stuff. When I got back again the bastards had torn the carpets up!

Excess wind. Now you don't have to blame the dog

Infant Folklore.

Throughout the civilized and uncivilised world

and in Watford as well children and the subject of procreation have served as a focus for superstitions folklore and even magic from the earliest of times. Here are the top ten such traditional themes.

1. A child born on a Friday will have poor health. This traditional eighteenth century English axiom was based on the cultural parallel that carts and carriages built on a Friday in the town-land of Leylandimum in Staffordshire were of a shoddy quality with problems such as wheels falling off, springs breaking, axles rumbling and the like. Indeed this theme will be familiar to anyone who bought a Morris Marina in 1978. It is also thought to be based on the fact that ancient midwives had Fridays off for day release unarmed combat lessons, and naked bear wrestling. As a result any woman giving birth on a Friday had only their hapless husband to help. This resulted in a lot of babies being dropped on the head, stood on by accident, mislaid, etc etc. This obviously had an effect on their future health.

2. Gypsies steal babies, especially blond haired ones. This is probably true as they have the reputation for stealing anything not bolted onto the earths core.

3. Holding a one day old baby and reciting a passage from Chaucer or Shakespeare is good luck. It only by good luck that you won't get covered in Puke or worse.

4. Passing a baby across the counter of a public bar is bad luck. This is an old Scottish folklore based on the fact that babies break wind when they smell alcohol. In times gone past Excise men in Dunoon would take

a baby with them as a sort of alcohol monitor. This worked OK for a while until the babies they took with them all developed bad diarrhoea with the attendant problems of contamination. The practice was stopped shortly after that.

5. Very young babies can predict earthquakes. This load of oriental bunkum comes from Japan where the goldfish theory has also been applied to babies. The rationale is that babies become restless before an earthquake and start mimicking goldfish. The reason that this is a load of cobblers has been proved by Dr Vince Sydney from the Institute of Assessments who found out that no matter where in Japan you are there are loads of restless babies. Also most Japanese babies look like goldfish.

6. Rubbing a baby girls face with rock salt promotes good looks. From Siberia this one and absolutely true, but only if you like your women having faces like half chewed toffees. Which Siberian men do.

7. Pregnant women are psychic. Another feed of nonsense from Central America, this is based on the general ravings that women impose on their often times hapless male partners. Quite a number of pregnant women are actually psychotic which is a whole different ballgame.

8. Female babies are more intelligent than boys. Aye right! Ask any of them how a turbocharger works!

9. Children born in November will never die of drowning. A crazy fable from the almost extinct Nukukuk tribe of Saudi Arabia who live at least two

thousand miles from the nearest open water.

11. Having sex standing up guarantees a male child. More like a slipped disc and a lifetime of severe sciatic back pain

The Problem Pages.

Many distraught dads have written letters exposing their naked desperation asking for advice and her are a few examples of common problems and appropriate solutions.

> Dear Doctor,
> My ten year old son Troy smokes ten Moroccan Collapsers a day, drinks Sea Shanty Lager, swears like a trooper and calls me and his mum by our first names. He has a string of 13 year old girlfriends and stays out until ten O'clock every night. What's gone wrong?
> Worried of Darlington

Dear Worried of Darlington
Don't worry, you have fatherhood well and truly cracked. What a wonderful start in life young Troy has had, sounds like he has a varied and well balanced social calendar. He obviously enjoys the simple pleasures in life that so many young people miss out on these days. Next thing you know he will be on Income Support and taking you and his mum on holiday to the Isle of Man with him. Well done!

Dear Doctor,
What a wee darling our twelve year old Timothy is. His quiet disposition is commented on by all our friends and he is so polite. Our one problem is that he works so hard at his homework to maintain his consistently top grades that we rarely see him in the evenings. What should we do?

Concerned of Coventry

Dear Concerned of Coventry,
Your Timothy is obviously unhinged and a bit of a worry. Get the little boyo out of the house a bit more, especially in the evenings. You could start by introducing him to the delights of derelict houses and street corner socializing. Make sure you act quickly though as experience shows that young lads like this usually grow up to be right pains in the arse. And politicians.

Dear Doctor,
My girlfriend is expecting triplets. What should I do?
Terrified of Wales

Dear Terrified of Wales,
Find out who done it first then get yourself down the allotment. Prepare well by reading this book and getting a big lock on the shed door. Take up deep sea fishing. Actually your life will never be the same again you poor bugger.

CHAPTER TEN

Case Studies

When the news is official and it is clear that you are going to be elevated to the grand and honourable status of 'The Dad' its all too easy to feel that you are out there on your own. How many men have felt they are the Columbus of the fatherhood ocean, littered with the shark like hazards of dealing with infant snot, toddler diarrhoea for the uninitiated and discharging adolescent ears. How many feel like the man whose dart game of life goes to double one every time and whose brand new trainers seek out the lurking dog turd of fatherhood misery even in broad daylight.

Don't despair, you are not the first and certainly will not be the last man trying to cope with stresses and strains the like of which can only be compared to that resisted by Dolly Parton's undergarments.

To help you put your own special circumstances into perspective a number of cases are presented for you to muse on and to demonstrate the wide spectrum of what psychologists laughingly call 'normality'.

Case One, Archie and Cynthia

Archie is a normal 34 year old healthy heavy drinker and keen fisherman whose girlfriend Cynthia (33) a barmaid, has just broken the news to him that she is engendered with foetus for the first time. Archie is absolutely delighted and immediately tells all his friends and neighbours of the good news.

Determined to take a full part in the pregnancy, Archie starts to walk around with a pillow stuffed up his jumper, complaining of backache and heartburn and eating cream cheese with walnuts and prunes until he is sick. Cynthia finds Archie's reaction somewhat bewildering as they have been having their differences for some time now.

Archie has suggested that Cynthia should have a water-birth and to have members of the Welsh National Women's herb and crystal club present ready to chant mantras and tap cymbals in harmony with her contractions and screams of mortal pain. Although Cynthia is not fully convinced she is coming to the conclusion that a minimal intervention confinement would suit her best and that she would consider having the baby in the midwife led unit at the local hospital.

Archie is in the psychiatric of Barlinne prison and has been there for the last 10 years.

Comment

When your partner tells you she is pregnant and you know there is no way the deed could have been done by you in person then its best to move all you kit lock, stock and barrel into a mates transit van or the YMCA hostel. Luckily for Archie there will be little change in his circumstances for the next 25 years and as long as he has a wall to talk to and a handful of pills to swallow and he will be quite happy.

Cynthia is now living with her new boyfriend who has a pony tail, drinks mineral water is well into lean cuisine and works in advertising.

Case two: Sammy and Tammy

Living in a remote farm near Perth where they breed horses, Sammy and Tammy, who are heavily into Country and Western culture, were delighted to be told that they were soon to be proud parents. Interestingly they seemed to be unaware of impending parenthood until the casualty doctor at the General Hospital tried to explain it to them when Tammy presented with excruciating stomach pains, which Sammy had put down to 'grass fever'.

Tammy thought that babies came from Mother Care and the casualty doctor might as well have tried to explain Einstein's theory of relativity to Sammy than to try and make him understand what was going on.

It was lucky then that in the next cubicle that there was a vet who was being treated for a badly crushed foot. The story was that, a keen pipe smoker, he had forgotten he had his Old Briar pipe fully charged with a fiery plug of 'Volcanic Jack's Black Shag' in his hand when he shoved it up a horses poop hole in the course of his duty. The horse rewarded him by the equivalent of equine tap dancing on his foot while farting sheets of solid flame and smoldering faeces all over a bystander.

Through the blinding pain he was able to describe the procreative process in terms of horse husbandry which the doe eyed couple could understand perfectly well. He inadvertently left them with the idea that human babies were little more than small hairless horses, a fact that was to have severe consequences. Eager to get back to their farm Tammy self discharged herself from hospital the next day but both Sammy and Tammy were back in town a bit sooner than they anticipated. They were summoned by the local senior health visitor and accused of gross negligence, physical and mental cruelty and behaviour likely to endanger the health of an infant.

At interview it transpired that the docile pair had taken the words of the vet literally and had set about feeding their son 'Dobbin' on mares milk, bran and oats. Their only concession to the vulnerability of their baby had been to rinse out the bucket they fed him from with Jey's fluid once a week.

Under close cross examination by the community midwife it became clear that no malice whatever had been intended by the loving parents and further that they actually had IQs in single figures. The boy (Dobbin) was taken into care (the nursery stable) and the parents sent for psychiatric examination.

Both parties responded well to therapy although it took Dobbin some time to get used to baby rice and milk and sixteen weeks later he still preferred to eat on the kitchen floor on all fours with his head and one hand in his bowl.

Comment

This remarkable story illustrates the simple fact

that the human brain has nothing at all to do with the process of having children. This is not surprising since the brain is at the opposite end of the body to where all of the baby making apparatus is.

Case Three, Gerald and Sophia

Born into military families both Gerald and Sophia had firm, clear views as to how their triplet sons, Gerald Junior, Sebring and Spencer were to be brought up. They adopted a strict regimen from birth for their children, inspecting their rooms on a daily basis and assigning duties and responsibilities at an early age.

By the age of five all the little darlings were self sufficient in the use of hand guns and pistols, knew the basics of unarmed combat and the interrogation of suspects and could survive in the wilds of Highland Scotland for a week without outside support.

During school holiday times they spent their days mounting mock assaults on their own house and on the physical persons of their parents. The punishment for failing to complete the mission was a good sound beating and being trussed up in an old sack in the cellar for two days. The prize for success was to be trussed up in an old sack in the cellar for two days. In either case the children were happy.

It was a natural continuation to their education when they all went to a fee paying school in the North York Moors which specialized in emphasizing the military aspect of life. Far from being happy, however, the triplets were disappointed with the lack of enthusiasm shown by their teachers for weapons training and live firing exercises, the psychology of interrogation and the art of field craft.

Determined that things should change they decided

to mount a coup d'etat on the school and take over, holding the headmaster to ransom for some proper military hardware. They chose morning assembly as a time to strike, and hit on a plan to destroy the French Block as well. They showed characteristic disregard for innocent bystanders.

They managed to coerce some sixth form boys to steal chemicals from the laboratories sufficient and appropriate to construct several explosive devices and a rocket.

On the allotted day the plan met with limited success. The French department did indeed sustain fire and smoke damage but by far the biggest impact was made on the headmasters office where the home made rocket exploded. Unfortunately the only casualties were the headmaster and his secretary who had significant difficulties explaining to their respective spouses how they had acquired flash burns to those parts of their bodies rarely exposed during the day and certainly not in the headmaster's office.

Despite covering their tracks well the triplets were apprehended by the Anti Terrorist Squad, returned to their parents with a bill for £147,000. The cost was partially offset by the fee paid by a National tabloid newspaper who ran the headline 'BOYS BOMBS BURN BUMS, SECRETARYS SEXY SECRET SHAME SCORCHED BY SAM 7'

Three years later all three lads were in the SAS after forging their birth certificates. They were dispatched into deepest Laos and despite the continued leaking of their position to the Laoatian rebel forces they survive quite happy to this day.

Comment

They type of behaviour exhibited by the triplets is referred to by psychologists as 'light the blue touch-paper and stand well back'. No matter what action the parents had taken it is unlikely that they would have been any less a hazard to society. In this regard it would have been better for all concerned if their father had has a bad 'testicles- caught-on-barbed-wire-fence' type accident before he had procreated.

Case four, Rick and Allanya.

Rick(45) and Allanya (47) are both unemployed professionals, that is neither of them had ever had a job in their lives. They got married in their early twenties but had no real plans to have children.

Rick got the chance of a trip to Barcelona to see a football match in 1967 but having got there he couldn't figure out a way to get back to Glasgow. Eventually he was deported from Spain in 1982 for being persistently vagrant and a hazard to public health. On his return home to his marital home in Cumbernauld on a Monday lunchtime he found a 15 year old youth tucking into beans and toast in the kitchen.

Three days later he asked the lad how long Bob a Job week was likely to last and didn't he think he was swinging the lead a bit by coming back three days on the trot. Only after a careful explanation was the confusion cleared up and the boy. Anton, identified as Ricks son.

Comment

Rick had become so detached from family life that

the part of his brain which controlled the recognition of his family had withered and died. This was hardly a problem as Allanya subsequently paid for a one way ticket for him back to Spain out of the family tax credits in the hope of never seeing him again. In this way family harmony was maintained.

Summary

These case studies highlight the full spectrum of family life concerning the role of the father in family life. Each case is normal in its own way and points to the imperative that a man's natural environment is not the delicatessen of Morrison's or the hair care counter at Boots.

No, a mans natural habitat is out on the wild side of society, standing his ground, protecting what is his, expanding his spheres of influence and taking rebuke from no one. Makes one think that a man's natural habitat is most likely on his allotment.

CHAPTER ELEVEN

Glossary

Whilst not extensive this glossary covers the main subject headings of which the average man should be conversant. importantly dropping a few of these words into the conversation at the right time could do your reputation as a man of understanding, sensitivity and second hand obstetrics a lot of good if you are in the company of women. Stay clear of conversations that concern post partum discharge, cracked nipples, sex after childbirth and maternity bras. These are subjects men have no part in understanding never mind discussing. It is akin to making a subjective comment about shoes your girl friend picks up in a posh shoe shop in Glasgow. Just leave it alone.

Bed Wetting
 This can be a particular problem for toddler and parent alike. From the toddlers point of

view it most likely is the normal adaptation to toilet training. From the fathers perspective it may be laziness, the habit of a lifetime or just exhaustion after having looked after the little darling for an interrupted 2 hour spell during the afternoon.

Conception
This is the miraculous biological event which, nine months later is guaranteed to turn you into a basket case in a remarkably short time. It can take place equally successfully in a fallopian tube or a Ford Fiesta.

Contraception
Any number of actions you could have taken nine months previously to prevent a man from becoming a basket case (see Conception). The most effective method is to keep your trousers on and drink a bottle of Vodka every day.

Contractions
What happens to your world when you are responsible for a child.

Contraptions
The painful squeezing that a woman inflict on a man's knackers as she screams in agony while grasping for something to hold on to.

Developmental assessment
Procedure where the health visitor checks

that, for example, for example, an average toddler by the age of two has his ears pierced, a wardrobe full of shell suits and hoodies, eats only crisps and drinks only coke, and knows and can use appropriately two four letter swear words.

Egg
Some young babies and children are allergic to eggs. Sperm, however, are not.

Epidural
An injection in the pregnant woman's back to relieve labour pain. This must be a psychological effect because, as every man knows, the baby does not come out of the woman's back.

Fertilization
The process where a woman prepares her body for becoming pregnant as fast as possible, thereby minimizing the time she needs to spend in the intimate company of a man. This includes wearing makeup, stockings, shaving her legs and not burping or breaking wind too much.

Baby monitor
A Nintendo DS, Game Boy, Playstation or X Box bought for an infant in the hope that it will keep them quiet. For about 10 minutes.

Gas and Air
> Babies breathe in air at one end and expel copious quantities of gas at the other. This is responsible for Global Warming and can be reduced by feeding your infant on a maximum of one Vindaloo a week.

Home Confinement
> What new mothers do to the father of their child for about six weeks after the baby is born to enlist help in looking after it.

Midwife
> An old woman who attends women in labour with the aim of reducing their pain and maximizing their male partners pain.

Parenting
> The act of a child training its parents to do exactly what it wants. If you are feeding your 5 month old chunks of Mars Bar at three O'clock in the morning then you have been well and truly parented.

Paediatrician
> A doctor who looks after babies and children. They are like a cross between an electrician and a pedicurist which shows how difficult a job it is.

Pethidine
> A powerful opium-like analgesic, given by

midwives to women in labour to take the pain away. Although most men experience the severe pain of birth on a daily basis doctors have never prescribed this to men.

Post Natal Depression.
The effect of having a baby on a mans bank account.

Special Care Baby Unit
A household kitchen containing a deep fat fryer with vegetable oil in it as opposed to lard.

CHAPTER TWELVE

The Practical Parenting Test

You have now completed reading this reference book and should be well versed in the theory of skills required to be an effective practical parent. how much you have taken in will depend on your thirst for knowledge in contrast to your thirst for Guinness. It will also depend on the degree of desperation you find yourself in.

To test your standing and acumen as a practical parent the following Practical Parenting Test has been devised. At the end of the questions is a key where you can work out how well or how badly you have done.

Good Luck!

1. Your partner informs you during a surprise candle-lit dinner for two that she is *'heavy with your child'*. Your response is.....

    a. Leap to your feet, grab the wine bottle from the table and smash it against the kitchenette wall, screaming at the top of your voice 'Ill kill the bastard who done it!' continuing to rant and rave for the next two hours.
    b. Leap to your feet, rush to your partner's side, burst into tears and spend the next twenty minutes proclaiming your undying devotion to her and your foetus.
    c. Raise your eyebrows and say 'Oh that's nice love, any more of that pink sauce for the kebab?'

2. You are enjoying a few can of Pils and some well deserved peace and quiet with your family by the side of a quaint, dreamy canal when your fifteen year old son, Errol, who has not stopped whining all bloody day gets very close to the edge. Do you...

    a. Reason with him that a rational approach based on cogent argument is a better tactic in achieving compromise in conflict situations rather than non stop utterances based on negativity and furthermore he should take care to avoid falling into the canal which could result in getting a

number of waterborne infections which could have severe consequences for his current and future health.
b. Threaten to punch his lights out if he doesn't shut his trap.
c. Sneak up behind him, kick him into the canal while singing 'What a sap, What a sap, What a sap' to the tune of 'Here we go.'

3. **What should you use to clean a three month old baby's face?**

    a. A clean square of cotton wool and some cool boiled water.
    b. Your whippet
    c. Your partner

4. **You are hosting a dinner party for some important business colleagues of your partner when your three year old daughter proudly announces that the most senior lady guest looks and smells like one of the monkeys she saw recently at London Zoo. Do you...**

    a. Openly scold your daughter, prolifically apologizing to your guest and punishing her by denying her the chance to go to Sunday School for the next three weeks and canceling her Ballet and dance lessons indefinitely.

b. Explain to your guest that she doesn't understand the implications of what she said and if it happens again she'll get a clip round the ear.
c. Guffaw loudly, getting your daughter to repeat the statement a few times and in between laughing uncontrollably state that 'Only children speak the real truth'.

5. **By the age of two and a half the average child should be able to...**

   a. Count to ten
   b. Count to ten, hop on one foot, draw a circle and ask to go to the toilet.
   c. Keep out of his dad's way or risk the consequences.

6. **Your sixteen year old daughter tells you that she is four and a half months pregnant by her 27 year old art teacher. Do you...**

   a. Burst into tears, sob uncontrollably and promising to stand by her whatever she wants to do.
   b. Find out what his salary is, where he lives and make a note to buy some more shotgun cartridges.
   c. Tell her there are two twenty foot ladders around the back of the shed if she wants to elope.

7. A heated argument develops in your house involving your wife, fifteen year old daughter and your twin twelve year old sons regarding the sleeping arrangements for when your mother in law comes to stay for a week. Do you...

   a. Spend three hours mediating between all parties going from room to room to try to find a compromise acceptable to everyone, putting your own feelings and opinions firmly in the background.
   b. Join in the fracas insisting that no matter what happens you will not give up your own bed and as far as you are concerned the stinking old bag can sleep in the bath.
   c. Quietly and imperceptibly disappear off down the allotment with a copy of the Racing Post to return only when the whole thing is sorted out.

8. Your eighteen year old son, Lawrence, asks you for your advice regarding his career and employment prospects. His strengths are cookery, fashion design, art and botany. Your career choice for him would be...

   a. A squaddie in the Parachute Regiment
   b. A features writer for Lovely House Weekly
   c. Dole Bludger like his dad.

9. Your 21 year old Punk Rocker/New Age Woman daughter, Hilda, brings a new boyfriend home and announces they are to marry. He is 6 feet 6 inches tall, blond and bronzed owns a Pacific Island and drives a Porsche. After you are left alone with him for a man-to-man chat which of the following do you ask him...

   a. Is there an allotment on the Island
   b. What the hell do you see remotely interesting in your daughter that the Dermatologist already had a look at.
   c. Can you drink a bottle of vodka and still urinate standing up.

10. Your children have all left home. After a social evening in the Clipper Bar in Lancaster Railway Station you reflect on your career to date as a father. You ask yourself the question 'Was it worth it?'. Your answer is...

    a. Yes
    b. No
    c. Don't understand the question

Now work out your score according to the following table

Q	Score	Your Score	Q	Score	You Score
1a	2		6a	1	
1b	1		6b	3	
1c	3		6c	2	
2a	1		7a	1	
2b	3		7b	2	
2c	2		7c	3	
3a	2		8a	2	
3b	3		8b	1	
3c	1		8c	3	
4a	1		9a	3	
4b	2		9b	3	
4c	3		9c	3	
5a	2		10a	1	
5b	2		10b	1	
5c	1		10c	3	
Total					

So, how did you do? Read on and find out.

0 to 10 points. You have the practical parenting skills of dry rot and the strength of character of a lettuce. How you have attained such little knowledge after studying this book is beyond comprehension. You will never make it as a dad

11 to 20 points. Not a bad attempt but you can do better. Concentrate on you skills of indifference to family matters and make your allotment the focus of your own personal universe.

21 points and more. Well done. You have parenting truly under your belt. See you down the allotment.

FEEDBACK

OK if you really feel the need to feedback then crack on. Email the author at mission@medactive.co.uk. And send money for the shed refurbishment.

Printed in Great Britain
by Amazon.co.uk, Ltd.,
Marston Gate.